Young Artists
Speak Out

*Passion, compassion and purpose
in the arts and education*

Peter Renshaw

Also see:
www.youngartistsspeakout.uk

Independently published.
Copyright © 2020 by Peter Renshaw
All rights reserved.
ISBN: 979-8-62-763212-4

Front cover image by Gar Powell-Evans

"What stands out for me in all Peter's work is his inquisitive approach, powerful insight and thoughtful observations. In this regard, Young Artists Speak Out is no exception. It makes you think, reflect and even more determined to drive change for and with young people, particularly those pursuing careers as socially engaged creatives. In addition to their powerful testimonies, we also get to hear more about Peter himself – his personal story, what drives him and his urgent call for action. This sets big challenges and asks questions of us all, particularly cultural and educational institutions with responsibility for training the artists of the future. We owe it young people to provide the supportive, conducive environments to drive their vision and social purpose forward. They deserve nothing less."

Matt Griffiths

CEO

Youth Music

FOREWORD
By Rineke Smilde

Once again, Peter Renshaw comes with a powerful publication that goes directly to the heart of the matter which has "kept him going", as he has often said himself for many years. This is the transformative role of the arts in society, which can be found in many places, but is nevertheless not seen sufficiently. Peter feels that giving the arts a strong voice is needed more than ever, especially in a world that seems to have lost its "moral compass". He argues that although the arts by themselves cannot resolve this, they can nevertheless play an important role in people's wellbeing and connect them to themselves and to others. This is a key observation when we find ourselves confronted by arguments that the arts cannot make any substantial difference as they remain in the margins of society.

Starting with a strong manifesto, the journey in the publication is clear. Peter makes his case in the most convincing way through letting young artists speak out. Their testimonies speak for themselves. They are the future and they are ready to make the world a better place.

Peter uses the keywords 'passion' and 'compassion', words which are outstandingly chosen for the artistic practices which are at the heart of change. Passion constantly underpins the excellence in the artist's artistic and social practice; it is needed for high-quality achievement in every aspect. Compassion goes hand-in-hand with this; it is needed in order to make a connection to be reciprocal, co-creative, in a real dialogue with the other. Empathy evolves into compassion in the artistic practice as soon as action comes into play. Compassion is an active given, and that is why it is so seamlessly connected to passion in making a difference in the situation and in contributing to wellbeing. Peter phrases this beautifully as the "synergy between passion, compassion and purpose" lying at the heart of social engagement, allowing people to flourish.

The fact that Peter underpins this with a strong biographical experience is moving and convincing. Haven't many of us had an experience which motivated us to do what we are doing? It happens all the time and that can be the wonderful result of biographical learning processes.

Last but not least, Peter points out what all of this means for the responsibility of higher education institutions. He argues that the gap between rhetoric and action remains considerable and a fundamental shift in mindset is required. This publication will contribute strongly to the latter goal. Institutions of higher arts education are invited to ask the fundamental question of their students: "Who am I as an artist and how can I contribute to society"? How can our institutions support the young artists in their journeys to become 'catalysts' who respond to the deep-seated needs of society? It is therefore to be hoped that institutions are interested in what these young artists bring with them as soon as they enter. That through being open, 'seeing them', respectfully acknowledging that they are the future and receiving the richness that this can entail, real change can begin. In that way institutions of higher arts education can enable their students, the future artists, to have an impact on people's wellbeing and sense of belonging. This will empower them to face the challenges of today's world and live in it with confidence.

Rineke Smilde
Professor of Lifelong Learning in Music
Hanze University Groningen – Prince Claus Conservatoire
University of Music & Performing Arts Vienna

CONTENTS

1
MANIFESTO

What young people have to say matters! In *Young Artists Speak Out* young creatives between the ages of 16 and 40 demonstrate how their socially engaged passion, together with their compassion and creative voice, can help to enhance the lives of others. Their sense of urgency, vitality, imagination and commitment shine through their testimonies, case studies and conversations.

Their voices form part of a rich intergenerational conversation, a circle of empathy, arising from a deep belief in the values underpinning our common humanity – respect, equality, freedom, integrity, openness, inclusion, diversity, cohesion, collaboration, creativity and generosity of spirit. The root of conversation is that it connects people. It draws people together, it respects difference, it sees commonalities, it crosses boundaries. A respectful conversation allows people to be heard. It has to provide a safe, non-judgemental space for people to listen and share their fears and vulnerabilities. A conversation that really connects goes beyond asking who, what, where and how. It thrives on the 'why' – on critical reflection and critical discourse. It reaches into the inner depth of people rather than remaining on the surface. Conversation then becomes a powerful catalyst for change and for action.

Young artists are angry. Many are now trying to address the injustices of the world – responding creatively to the anxiety, vulnerability, loneliness and sense of alienation of those people struggling to cope in a harshly divided world where the 'system' fails to meet their needs. I share their anger. So many of our systems, the bedrock of a humane society, seem to be broken or are severely dysfunctional. Health, social care, education, criminal justice, immigration, the environment – each raises major challenges for government, for local services, for the business community, for cultural and educational institutions and for the charity sector. But this deep crisis has increasingly unlocked the collective imagination, the hearts and minds of many creative young people who are determined to mobilise their activism and re-imagine their relationship with the world. They recognise that their activism should come from how they perceive who they are, from their beliefs and values, and from how they see the world.

Their collective voices have become a force to reckon with. These young artists have the skill, motivation and will to engage with the world directly rather than wait for cultural and educational institutions to act. Their actions provide a beacon of hope that might inspire others in the arts community to become more socially engaged.

The assumption underlying this manifesto is that all cultural and higher arts education institutions, together with their decision makers, should be working collectively to ensure that young and emergent artists have the skills, values and attitudes to meet the challenges confronting society today. Most importantly, these institutions need to listen to and work with those young people who already have a strong sense of social engagement. It is critical that these young artists are involved in the processes that will eventually shape their futures, respecting them as active learners and knowledge creators. Their voices compel us to listen and to act. They give us hope as they cut through the conservative, bureaucratic constraints of institutions, harnessing their vision and demonstrating the power of the arts to lift the human spirit and address the needs of people within a wide variety of social and cultural contexts. Their determination demands a sense of urgency from politicians and leaders of cultural institutions.

2
PROVOCATION

It is clear from the Manifesto underpinning *Young Artists Speak Out* that in the future much of the cutting-edge socially engaged action lies in the hands of those young leaders who have the drive, vision, skills and initiative to make an impact on the world. It would be hoped that cultural and higher arts education institutions would also be committed to preparing young artists to take a more active role in society. But at present social engagement remains largely on the periphery of these institutions despite the rhetoric about the important responsibility of the artist in society. In general there is an apparent lack of will to realign priorities and bring social engagement in from the margins. From my experience of working in many different cultural institutions over many years, there is an enormous gap between the rhetoric and the action.

One of the aims of *Young Artists Speak Out* is to provide a platform for young creatives, social activists working in challenging contexts, to become part of a wider conversation – one in which individual aspirations, collective energy and pragmatic idealism can become a source of inspiration and motivation for others. Like Greta Thunberg, the remarkable 17-year-old Swedish climate change activist, and many others like her, these young artists wish to create a better future. They are keen to address the problems caused by recent generations – environment, lack of wellbeing, social ills, the impact of aggressive capitalism, for example. They see the world from a new perspective and are not afraid of making radical changes. Their spirit of hope is contagious as they take the action they feel is necessary to respond to the many social challenges of our time. They refuse to hide behind a veil of cynicism because they know that their creative engagement can have a transformational impact and consequence. They know that the systemic change required in cultural and higher arts education institutions will not happen without individual change, involving a major shift in the personal attitudes and values of teachers and students. To effect change there has to be a fundamental shift in the individual and collective mindset of these institutions.

The young artists speaking out in this polemic are exemplary role models. Their actions raise several fundamental questions that need to be addressed urgently:

- In what ways might young activists and higher arts education institutions establish a dynamic dialogue to ensure that social engagement becomes a priority in the preparation and continuing development of artists?

- What structures and resources outside current institutions are necessary to facilitate and strengthen the social impact of young engaged activists and nurture them as potential social leaders?

- In what ways might cultural and political leaders accept greater responsibility for recognising and nurturing socially engaged artists for their commitment to shaping a more inclusive, compassionate society?

- What action needs to be taken to bring socially engaged artists in from the margins to a more central strategic position in the cultural field?

- In what ways can more young artists be galvanised to find the passion, compassion and sense of purpose to make a difference in the world?

- What action can be taken to ensure that the next generation of artists has the artistic strength, vision and motivation to create a world in which engaging in the arts enhances the quality of people's lives?

- In what ways can cultural institutions be activated to produce a socially engaged workforce that responds creatively and responsibly to the diverse challenges of a world in constant flux?

It is up to those working with young artists to formulate the answers and responses to these ongoing challenges.

3

PASSION, COMPASSION AND PURPOSE: A PERSONAL PERSPECTIVE

WHY DO I FEEL THE VOICES AND ACTIONS OF YOUNG PEOPLE MATTER?

What drives me in my continuing desire to connect to the voices of young artists? What is the source of my motivation? A question that I've often been asked! The testimonies, case studies, poems and conversations that form the core of *Young Artists Speak Out* demonstrate that creative engagement and social activism are very much alive, and increasingly more and more young artists see them as a key part of their mission in life. Their passion for what they do, their compassion for people and their strong sense of purpose are bound together, making them a formidable force for change. The synergy between passion, compassion and purpose lies at the heart of social engagement – this is a sine qua non, and conditions need to be created that ensure it is allowed to flourish.

For me, this reciprocal relationship between passion, compassion and purpose has grown organically over many years. It has needed time, space and life experience to mature, strengthen and come together as an intentional driving force. But once passion and compassion started working together towards a common end, the flow of energy had a dynamic power of its own. Life was never quite the same again.

The roots of my commitment to the activism of young people go back to the 1960s when a wave of social movements began to shape the values of students the world over. The wider political context was fraught with growing turbulence and protest: civil rights in the USA; the campaign for nuclear disarmament; anti-war movements arising from conflicts in Vietnam, Northern Ireland, Africa and Israel-Palestine; anger at social injustice and inequality in France; cries for freedom of speech in Prague, Warsaw and former Yugoslavia – to name but a few.

1968 was the vintage year for student protests in Europe. I was in my early thirties and witnessed protests breaking out everywhere: first Paris Nanterre University, then the Universities of Amsterdam and Nijmegen in The Netherlands, the Free University in Berlin, the Universities of Stockholm and Madrid, and the London School of Economics, Hornsey College of Art and Brighton College of Art in the UK. These protests need to be seen in the wider context of student and youth politics and activism, and to growing pressures towards social and educational change. The focus of student discontent was primarily on the relevance of the curriculum to contemporary society, the need to restructure courses, perceived outdated teaching methods, and the need for student representation and greater student participation.

This was a very formative time for anyone involved in education. Having taught History in a London comprehensive school for three years, I moved into teacher education, first lecturing in History and then in Philosophy of Education. The social turbulence of the time did not leave me unaffected. In 1968 I was supported by the Principal of my College of Education to encourage the students to become more active and socially aware. At the time I was writing my MPhil thesis on *The Concept of a College of Education* and this resulted in my being invited to attend a conference at the University of Bristol, organised by the Council of Europe, on The Reform of Teacher Education. A small group of lecturers, led by Harry Rée, Professor of Education at the University of York, felt the main thrust of the Conference was not radical enough in its discussion of the quality and relevance of teacher education. This splinter group decided to form the Society for the Promotion of Educational Reform through Teacher Training (SPERTTT), which directed its protest and proposals at colleges and departments of education.

SPERTTT became active throughout the country bringing together students, lecturers, teachers, parents, administrators, councillors and the educational press to discuss the most meaningful and pragmatic ways of reforming the teacher education system. Its findings became the basis of a book, *Dear Lord James: A critique of teacher education* (Burgess, 1971), which was submitted to the Committee of Inquiry on *Teacher Education and Training* (DES, 1972), chaired by Lord James, Vice-Chancellor of the University of York. My own contribution focused on the reform of the teacher education curriculum. One statement in the chapter could serve as a thread throughout my life in education:

> *The children of today are entering a dynamic regenerative society, in which the pace of technological advance is accelerating, bringing in its wake a range of new social and economic demands, new organisational structures, new concepts, attitudes, systems, roles and patterns of behaviour. The needs of such a society must be reflected in any teacher-education programme. Colleges cannot afford to be bound by obstructionist traditions; the curriculum should be continually reappraised in the light of ever-changing conditions.* (Renshaw, 1971, pp.81-82)

SPERTTT created a framework for harnessing the energy and commitment of those student teachers wanting change. Many were frustrated with a system they regarded as outmoded, and they saw their involvement in SPERTTT as an opportunity to voice their views in a growing national conversation. It was also an opportunity for me to help choreograph this conversation at both a national and local college level. The student voice gradually grew in strength and clarity, quickly leading to greater student representation and participation in colleges.

In a sense this sowed the seeds of my commitment to valuing and listening to the student voice, a commitment that I nurtured when I moved on to teach at the University of Leeds Institute of Education (1970-1975) and then as Principal of the Yehudi Menuhin School (1975-1984). At the School I initiated a strong programme of social engagement involving students performing in hospices, psychiatric hospitals, Broadmoor high security hospital, institutions for young offenders, homes for the elderly, centres for people with learning difficulties, and a Yorkshire coal mining community. These challenging contexts entailed my being very supportive and open to the ear of the young musicians.

In 1984, I pioneered an innovative programme in performance and communication skills (PCS) at the Guildhall School of Music & Drama together with Peter Wiegold, the Artistic Director. Initially this began as a three-year pilot project, evaluated by the Centre for Applied Research in Education at the University of East Anglia. It then went through different phases of development: a full-time one-year postgraduate course, the Guildhall Ensemble, a modular CPD programme, establishing the Department of Performance and Communication Skills, and later the creation of Guildhall Connect, a Master's degree in Leadership and a new BA in Performance and Creative Enterprise.

These extensive developments have been central to the main thrust of my reforming journey in the world of conservatoires, a journey that continues to the present day especially through various publications drawing on practice-based or action research. (See Renshaw, 2005, 2010, 2011, 2013, 2017) Throughout this time the student voice has always been seen as critical to the twin pillars of this challenge to the system – the development of socially engaged practice and creative collaborative practice. The young artists, the young creatives and teachers driving this work are the future, and they must be given the space and opportunity to shape a future that reflects the norms and values of a changing world.

WHAT IS THE SOURCE OF MY MOTIVATION?

In the 1950s I was a chorister and violinist in the National Youth Orchestra. My life was rooted in Classical music. In 1954 I gained a Choral Exhibition to Gonville and Caius College, Cambridge, where I read Music and History. But it was only during the three years after leaving university that I became more acutely aware of the social injustice that permeates society. Two years in the army serving as a Signals officer on an airbase in Singapore, followed by a year in industry, was the springboard of my commitment to education and social engagement.

In 1961 one seminal moment totally changed my way of looking at music-making. I was 25 years old. It was World Refugee Year, a time when Europe, through various agencies was trying to ameliorate the tragic conditions of over 100,000 displaced refugees who had been left bereft without country, home or future. During the Cold War of 1947 to 1991 the Eastern Bloc countries comprised the Soviet Union and its East European satellite states of East Germany, Poland, Czechoslovakia, Hungary, Romania, Bulgaria and Albania. The break-up of the Eastern Bloc began in 1956 with the Hungarian Revolution. This triggered a wave of refugees, many of whom fled to Austria, where they struggled to survive in old army barracks, converted stables, ex-Nazi youth camps, disused factories, decaying hotels and sometimes in ex-concentration camps. Both young and old were caught up in this cycle of neglect. They had little opportunity for work and they suffered from loss of hope, acute sickness like tuberculosis, and a lack of will to cope with normal life.

During World Refugee Year, as a trainee teacher at Oxford, what caught my imagination were those students who went out to Austria to build houses for the many refugees living in camps. This was obviously a very basic need but I could also see the potential of enriching their lives through sharing live music with them. So I approached the United Nations Association (UNA), which was coordinating the various building projects, and suggested that I bring together a group of versatile musicians who would live in the camps and give concerts to the children, families and elderly people. UNA was immediately enthusiastic about the idea and I quickly set about finding musicians who had the skills and attitudes to meet the social and musical challenges ahead. I was also fortunate to gain the generous support of the BBC, who gave me free access to its music library. An added bonus was Ford Motor Company donating a red van for our trip – my first venture into sponsorship! In the summer of 1961, our group of 11 musicians went out to Austria for a month, living and performing in a number of camps, notably near Linz (Lager 59, Wegscheid and Asten), Graz (Feffernitz) and Salzburg. In the following summer we repeated this tour with 22 musicians culminating in a fundraising concert in Vienna.

Out of the 60 concerts in the camps one particularly stands out. On our first tour we took a string quartet, led by Sheila Nelson, to play to a sick 80-year-old lady, Olga, in her small room in a TB sanatorium high up in the mountains outside Salzburg. Olga was a Hungarian who had been a professional violinist in Vienna before the War but had not heard any live music for 15 years. This was a very important occasion for her, which was recognised by the UNA staff working in the area. Knowing a little about her musical background we planned the programme accordingly to include Bartók, Kodály and Haydn's 'Emperor' Quartet. In the middle of the slow movement of the Haydn, which is a set of variations on the theme of the Austrian national anthem, the atmosphere became very intense and emotional as the music awakened many memories for Olga. She was very tearful as she was transported back into her musical life in Vienna. We only just managed to keep playing as we struggled to cope with our own emotions.

Looking back on this deeply moving experience I have often thought it was the pivotal musical moment in my life. It totally transformed my way of looking at making music. So much of what has happened subsequently hangs on the memories and feelings of that particular afternoon. It made me acutely aware of the potential power of music in intimate settings, a power that can generate a resonance and poignancy not always achieved in the more impersonal space of a concert hall or cathedral. This memory remains very much alive within me and on many occasions has confirmed my view that for a musical performance to make sense, it has to connect to its audience and to the context in which it is taking place.

But this experience also reinforced a decision I had made a few years earlier whilst studying at Cambridge – that I would never become a professional violinist or singer because I didn't want my love of music destroyed by the cynicism often encountered in the profession. Professional musicians can so easily erect a defensive barrier that seemingly protects them from their deeper feelings and love of music – something readily lost through the harsh realities of the workplace. The sheer joy of making music in the refugee camps, the direct engagement and response of the audience convinced me that I would remain a highly committed musician but always as an 'amateur' trying to retain the spirit of loving what one is doing.

PASSION, COMPASSION AND PURPOSE

What did I learn from this powerful experience of making music in the refugee camps? First, what stood out was my passion for music and for people. But on further reflection I became increasingly aware that an unfettered engagement in any activity can lead to an unhealthy self-absorption. The whole refugee camp experience left me with a deep conviction that when working in any kind of social context, passion cannot stand alone – it has to go hand in hand with compassion. Here I'm not talking about a sentimental, guilt-induced attitude of 'doing good' or of playing at being 'lady bountiful'. No! It is a belief that one's passion lives within a spirit of care, warmth, empathy, respect, trust, listening and understanding other people's worlds – qualities that are integral to compassion. This means that in any human context, whether it is a school, hospital, residential home, church, prison, factory or business, everyone should be treated with respect and compassion. This principle applies equally to life in all cultural organisations such as orchestras, opera houses, dance companies, theatres, arts centres, conservatoires and academies.

But passion and compassion can be uneasy bedfellows. Achieving a synergy between the two is not straightforward as they are both strong forces in their own right. A passion for music, for example, can be all-consuming, carrying with it a self-contained inner emotional life that might well find it unnecessary to look beyond itself – except of course to an audience which could then be seen as just another means of reinforcing life within a self-referential bubble. Similarly, an intense purposeful passion for people, however well-intentioned, can also lead to a single-track disposition trapped within an equally closed social and psychological bubble.

How can this seeming dilemma be resolved? I think in the first instance by recognising and understanding the nature of the possible tension between one's passion and compassion. In my case this is between music and people, but for others this could imply any activity to which one is fully committed and the human context in which it takes place. Although maintaining a balance between the two constitutes a challenge, in an important respect both passion and compassion feed off each other. In the arts there can be a powerful synergy between the artistic impetus, the creative force, and the moral imperative underpinning a person's actions.

This connection between passion and compassion is fundamental to what it is to be human, but time and again it is trampled on by forces seemingly beyond our control: for example, economic constraints, mechanistic target-driven systems and social inequality. But when one encounters passion and compassion working together in full flow the results can be extraordinary, and they readily enrich and transform people's lives. Perhaps most importantly, they are unlikely to achieve this without being inextricably linked to a person's sense of purpose. The testimonies, case studies and conversations in Chapters 4 to 9 that form the backbone of *Young Artists Speak Out*, demonstrate the power of the synergy between an individual's or group's passion, compassion and purpose.

4

VALUING THE VOICE OF YOUNG PEOPLE: DIFFERENT PERSPECTIVES, A UNITED VOICE

IN CONVERSATION

Connecting conversations lie at the heart of *Young Artists Speak Out*. All the young creatives, social activists, have entered this collective process through their testimonies, poems, interviews and group discussions. They were given the space and time for their voices to be heard without judgement and without consequences. What they have to say can be seen as a source of knowledge and expertise, which can well serve as an inspiration for other young people engaged in the arts. Their voices need to be listened to and supported, especially as their power can come through their interaction with others, including older people. From my experience, intergenerational conversation based on trust and mutual respect is one of the richest forms of communication and one of the most effective ways of understanding different ways of seeing the world.

This book is built around conversations, personal testimonies and poetry from young creatives and artists working with a wide range of people in different social settings. The age range lies between 16 and 40 years of age. Some of the contributions focus on how engaging in the arts, in the creative process, has enhanced and changed the lives of the artists. Others demonstrate the transformational value of their creative work in other people's lives in a variety of different contexts, especially in the areas of mental health, prisons, refugees and migrants.

Choreographing these many conversations has been a sensitive process and all the contributors have been extremely responsive to the challenge, which inevitably has raised deep personal questions of value, belief and motivation. In the interviews and discussions people were asked two open questions:

> How do you feel about your life at the moment? What are some of the key issues that you are concerned about?

> In what ways does writing, making music and engaging in creative projects make a difference to your life?

For the people writing personal testimonies they were given the following guidelines:

> A brief description of your own background. Why do you do what you do? What drives you? What is the source of your motivation? What are your values?

> A piece describing your feelings about the state of the world at the moment and how this reflects on your own life and work.

> A piece describing how engaging in the arts and creative projects can make a qualitative difference to young people's lives.

Their responses are at the core of this book. Some of the testimonies had to be edited for reasons of clarity and brevity but their core content has remained intact. The themes arising from these testimonies and conversations were understandably wide-ranging and reflect many of the key issues confronting society at the moment. For example:

- Identity: LGBTQ+, gender, race, social class
- Belonging: sense of 'family', community, kinship, gang
- Mental health: anxiety, depression, anger, alienation, insecurity, loneliness, sense of connection or disconnection through social media
- Criminal justice: prevention, prison and rehabilitation
- Migration and refugees: social and political activism
- Digital technology: creative use
- School curriculum: creativity and the arts

The relevance and resonance of these issues were explored with great honesty and concern from many different perspectives, and they present a major challenge to those young artists who wish to make a positive difference in the world.

RESPECTING THE VOICE OF YOUNG PEOPLE

One thread that ran through these conversations with different groups of young people was their deeply felt need to be listened to and respected. They spoke with a united voice, although rooted in very different contexts.

The two poems below, written by Helen[1], illustrate the power of the written word – words that can hardly be ignored. I first met Helen through the Making Tracks and Young Producers' programmes of The Irene Taylor Trust[2]. After an illuminating conversation with her (included in Chapter 6), Helen produced

---

[1] For reasons of privacy Helen's surname has been omitted.
[2] www.irenetaylortrust.com

these poems, drawing on her reflections at critical stages of her complex life. For her, writing and making music have become her lifeline. The creative process has enabled her voice to be heard. What matters now is that Helen's voice is listened to and what she has to say is valued.

Haunted – poem by Helen

I find myself trapped in a downwards spiral
Born a child of the storm, I return to my roots
I seek refuge in the eye of the hurricane
Haunted by ghosts of the past

Sadness envelopes me; a blanket of comfort
The weight on my shoulder familiar
Shame, however, suffocates me slowly
Tightening around my neck with every breath

I bite my tongue as another doctor tells me
To "forgive" myself; I was only four
I can't "forgive" myself, as a twenty year old
When, during my nightmares, I still can't stop them

Never too late – poem by Helen

For too many years, I was afraid
Too many years were taken away
I'm no longer in imminent danger
Yet, I still catch myself running

I grew up, physically, fast
And was criticised, equally fast
By the standards of a woman
Rather than a young girl

I eventually noticed a theme;
I'm ugly when I'm fat
Ugly when I'm thin
Disgusting on the inside

I decide now is the time
To ask the difficult questions
And expect a proper answer
To rebel against my past

I rebel by loving others
By looking people in the eye
I rebel by accepting help
By not letting myself die

The only school I visited during my nine months of conversations was Warren School in Chadwell Heath, the London Borough of Barking and Dagenham. Drum Works[3], an Artistic Associate of the Barbican, had been leading drumming sessions there for four years, with funding from a major funding body, Youth Music[4]. I had a full discussion with 25 fifteen- to sixteen-year olds who offered a fierce critique of the pressurised, mechanistic, target-driven system that now underpins, or masquerades as, 'education'. They couldn't see the point of being "filled with information geared to testing and examinations", rather than being taught "how to learn". They felt their views on what is happening in society are not valued or listened to. They wanted to be given the opportunity "to get out into the world", as they felt trapped by an educational system that puts them in boxes where they are told to act in certain prescribed ways. Little attempt is made to enable them to put their own authentic stamp on their learning.

---

[3] www.drumworks.co.uk
[4] www.youthmusic.org.uk

In stark contrast Drum Works sessions in the school were seen as "lessons for life" – "everyone's opinions and contributions are valued equally" within a culture of shared learning, mutual respect, trust and working harmoniously together. Its whole approach is supportive and interactive, which builds up a strong team spirit. The students also valued the opportunity to learn "transformative skills that can be applied to life outside school, such as communication, sharing, supporting and interacting with others". Within the group there was a strong sense of "belonging to a family". Not surprisingly, the students questioned why these qualities, skills and attitudes can't be fostered in the normal classroom. They want to learn, but only in an environment that makes sense to them and that resonates with their perspective on life.

This perspective on learning and education is shared by Daisy Swift, Learning Director of Wigmore Hall, a major chamber music venue in London[5]. Daisy's role focuses on schools, young people and the wider community, but her department also includes the work of Music for Life: a pioneering programme for people living with dementia and their families, friends and carers. Daisy's testimony, *The paradox of hyperconnectivity, and the power of music to connect us – for real*, presents a strong case for valuing the voice of young people, especially through creative collaborations in the arts. (Daisy's voice is heard again in Chapter 5 on the Arts, Identity and Belonging.) From Daisy's testimony:

> *I believe the arts have the power to engender equality; to enable expression and exploration of the self, of ideas; can give voice to those who don't have a platform to be heard; and can create a sense of kinship, of community (...) I'm worried about how disconnected we are as a society, about the frankly terrifying political context*

---

[5] www.wigmore-hall.org.uk/learning

we're in. But! – I'm also excited and inspired by young people who are rising up, raising their voices. And I believe that together we can make change.

(...) We're often told we're not the activists of former generations, and I think it's because we feel disempowered, disillusioned, uncertain. I know I do. We are grappling with our place in society, and it's hard to know how to effect change when what we're dealing with is climate change, economic crashes, political crises – it quite literally feels like the end of the world.

I think there's a change coming: young people are marching, speaking out, changing what they eat, thinking about what they buy and where they buy it. In some ways young people are greater participators than ever before. They aren't merely consumers of content; through the internet they have become creators. And they can use that to become participators, co-creators, change makers.

A cri de coeur for harnessing 'youth voice' can also be heard in the testimony of Osnat Ritter, an educator and activist from Israel/Palestine. On refusing to join the army for military service Osnat, now regarded as a 'betrayer' in Israel, founded the Tachles Art Centre for Palestinian and Israeli youth in Haifa[6]. Subsequently Osnat has worked with children in Senegal and with marginalised groups in Israel and the UK. With a focus on critical pedagogy, she has facilitated conflict groups, workshops in schools and after-school clubs, as well as building campaigns and community activities.[7] Deeply disturbed by the gross injustices in the world, Osnat, a pragmatic idealist, offers a ray of hope especially if young people are given a platform to speak out. Her views are developed further in Chapter 8 in the context of

---

[6] www.ocritter.wordpress.com/tachles-art-centre-haifa/
[7] www.springboardyouth.com

the Arts, Refugees and Migrants. From Osnat's testimony:

> *Listening to the news all around the world is pretty depressing – children being separated from their parents and sent to jail, young asylum seekers committing suicide due to lack of support from the government and the long journey to gain recognition from the Home Office in the UK. There isn't much hope for us young people out there in the big world. It seems like wherever you go the voices of young people are being silenced; our voices have been taken and our stories are often being told by others. (…)*

> *Feelings of anger, pain, apathy and frustration often take over my daily life – feeling angry for all the injustices happening around us, feeling apathy as I continue my life although these injustices take place so close to me, pain for the suffering that is being caused and frustration for not being able to change it. Yet, I remain an advocate for small changes and prioritise the importance of voice, and youth voice in particular.*

THE ARTS, CREATIVITY AND EDUCATION

One of the recurring themes in *Young Artists Speak Out* is the need to strengthen the place of the arts and creativity in education. One of the most pertinent observations about the contribution the arts can play in our troubled world came from Katie Bunting, who at the time of writing was a 2nd Year student on the BA course in Performance and Creative Enterprise (PACE) at the Guildhall School of Music & Drama.

> *In 2018, the world is in a state of division. Brexit is pulling countries, families, and people's lives apart by encouraging divisive attitudes and an ethos of exclusion. Donald Trump is telling women they are unimportant, religious groups that they are unwelcome and refugees they are unwanted. The leader of the free world is*

spreading hate across the globe and we in Britain are removing ourselves from allies and the sense of inclusion and support that can tackle such divisive energy. Our generation will be the poorest in fifty years. Rent is extortionate, wages are low, jobs are scarce and politicians' time is spent debating an issue we voted, almost unanimously against, under the leadership of a party we definitely didn't vote for. It feels uncomfortable to be coming into adulthood in a country pursuing an agenda that I don't believe in, but that I will struggle to afford to stay a part of.

In 2018 we should be finding ways to save the planet, supporting the development of young people and caring for our elderly. Instead we are having to vote for parties still debating a housing crisis, tackling poverty, and the survival of the NHS. It's like no progress has been made since the era of Victorian politics! I believe as young people we should have the freedom to think optimistically about the future and to act on what we would like the world our children grow in to be. Now though, I feel there is too much to worry about in the present for there to be space for that freedom of thought. Our future is being dictated by what is happening now, and so much of it is not what we want.

But this for me is where art comes in. Art is what tackles division and fosters inclusion. Art creates a space for optimism about the future to be found. And most importantly art is able to give a voice to anyone who wants to share their thoughts or opinions, regardless of age, gender, race, religion or circumstance. The most important thing that growing up with the space and skills to express myself creatively gave me was a belief that my voice was worth listening to and that what I had to say was important. I wouldn't want to live in a world where young people were told anything other than this.

We should be fostering leaders who believe in equality and inclusion, who are able to see strength in everyone, and who can connect genuinely on a human level with those they're leading. On the most basic level, being involved in drama or music ensembles teaches this. It also instils skills that may seem basic but are imperative to the future leaders of our country, such as the ability to hold a conversation, make eye contact with someone, express a point clearly, work as a team, or empathise with the situation of another person. All these are attributes I have and which I first encountered, and continue to develop, in drama education (though I'm sure the same can be said for music).

Another former Guildhall PACE student, Luce Howell, echoes the views of Katie about the importance of the arts in schools.

Fundamentally, I feel the interpersonal values the arts can provide for young people, on both a social and human level, speak out strongly. The state of our current political climate can feel like a terrifying place in history; there is rising epidemic rates of poverty, mental health issues and widespread oppression in just the UK alone. Equipping a rich artistic community in and outside of school offers a platform for discussion among young people; it can provide tools for thinking both critically and sensitively on their own personal struggles, and the struggles they may encounter socially.

In my own personal view, I believe firmly in the transformative power the arts can have in our human lives. It is not only integral to our cultural needs to question the fabric of how our society changes, but it also provides laughter, enjoyment, capacities for love and healing. There is a guttural sense of anger in me over how government bodies fail to recognise this; that our system

> *at its core is hungry to push art out of education, in favour of standardised testing and exam-based models.*

It is not surprising that the blindness of recent governments has generated so much anger within the arts community both in the UK and in other countries. For example, over 20 years ago in England, the National Advisory Committee on Creative and Cultural Education (NACCCE, 1999), chaired by Sir Ken Robinson, published its seminal report *All Our Futures: Creativity, Culture & Education.* The Report made a strong case for developing creative and cultural education, emphasising the importance of fostering creativity across the curriculum. In its initial statement the Report states that:

> *By creative education we mean forms of education that develop young people's capacities for original ideas and action: by cultural education we mean forms of education that enable them to engage positively with the growing complexity and diversity of social values and ways of life. We argue that there are important relationships between creative and cultural education, and significant implications for methods of teaching and assessment, the balance of the school curriculum and for partnerships between schools and the wider world. (ibid., p.6)*

The main findings of this Report echo those embedded in two earlier reports concerning the significance of the arts and creativity in education. First, the landmark Report, *The Arts in Schools* (1982), produced for the Calouste Gulbenkian Foundation and chaired by its Director, Peter Brinson. This set a benchmark for the place of the arts in the curriculum within the maintained sector of education. Then 15 years later Arts Council England (ACE) published a further Report, *Leading through Learning* (1997) on the education and training policy for the English Arts Funding System. In its preface Sir Christopher Frayling, then Chair of the ACE's Education and Training Panel, stated that:

> *The arts enrich the lives of most people in England, generating employment, stimulating creativity and providing enjoyment. The skills people acquire through studying and practicing the arts are among those most needed in the modern workplace; while involvement in the arts not only provides opportunities for personal fulfilment but also promotes a sense of community.*

> (Quoted by Pauline Tambling, former joint-CEO of Creative & Cultural Skills, in her reflections on '20 years of cultural learning in England', in Cultural Learning Alliance *Newsletter*, 30 September, 2019, pp.2-3.) [8]

Despite the strength of these reports, the case for the arts and creativity has been severely eroded by the government's commitment to an education dominated by the STEM subjects of Science, Technology, Engineering and Maths. More recently there has been a fightback to strengthen the arts on the curriculum, so that STEM becomes STEAM. In its first Briefing Paper, the Cultural Learning Alliance, in conjunction with NESTA (the National Endowment for Science, Technology and the Arts) made a joint statement:

> *Cultural education is integral to the happiness of our children and their families; to the strength of our communities and to the economic progress and international standing of our country. It turns STEM into STEAM: it fires the curriculum and creates individuals who are more inquisitive, persistent, imaginative, disciplined and collaborative.*
> (Cultural Learning Alliance, *Briefing Paper No.1*, 2017, p.2)

---

[8] www.culturallearningalliance.org.uk.

There is now a growing urgency to ensure that the arts, culture and creativity form a substantive part of the education of every young person. This is the main thrust of the Durham Commission on Creativity and Education, published in 2019.[9] The Commission examined the place that creativity and creative thinking should play in the education of young people. It was set up in response to the strength of opinion across the business, education and public sectors that young people are entering a world in which their knowledge and skills are no longer sufficient.

In the Foreword to the Report Sir Nicholas Serota, Chair of the Commission, made the following key observations:

> *The faster pace of change requires an evolution in how we think, and how we think about education and the way children learn. Our current, knowledge-based system only goes part of the way towards equipping young people with the skills that will give them the confidence and resilience to shape our own path through life. They need to make the most of our human capacity for imagination and critical judgment, especially with our ever-greater dependency on technology and artificial intelligence. They need to exercise creativity.*

> *There remains a misconception that creativity is solely the province of the arts. This is not true. Creativity exists in all disciplines. It is valued by mathematicians, scientists and entrepreneurs, as well as by artists, writers and composers.*

> *The Commission believes that the arts make an invaluable contribution to the development of creativity in young people. We are therefore deeply concerned about the reduction of status of arts subjects including*

---

[9] www.artscouncil.org.uk/publication/durham-commission-creativity-education

art and design, dance, drama and music within schools that has followed the introduction of the EBacc in secondary education.

As widely recognised, creativity is the driver of economic growth and innovation. Especially in the last 10 years, our national economy has been boosted by the success of the creative industries. Such success will only continue so long as we can ensure that young people are given the opportunity to experience and develop the skills in art, drama, music, design, craft and digital awareness that are the foundation of the creative industries.

Across the country, the Commission has found many moving examples of the ways in which creativity has fired young people's imagination, empathy and the ability to effect positive change. Creativity often depends on collaboration, or on sharing insight and experience, and can be a powerful catalyst for civic engagement, changing communities for the better.

Many leaders across business and civic society told us how creativity helps young people to generate ideas, to apply their knowledge to new circumstances, to have the courage to fail and try again. Many others talked about the value of creativity in terms of personal resilience and happiness. At a time when the mental health of children and young people is of concern, there is ample evidence of the value and importance of creativity in supporting wellbeing. Young people can find strength, inspiration, consolation and community in their shared experience of creativity. (ibid., pp.5-8)

COMMUNITY, CREATIVITY AND COLLABORATION

The last two observations are especially relevant to the thinking and practice of the young creatives who are sharing their experience in *Young Artists Speak Out*. But many would go further as they feel very strongly about the current state of the world in which so many political leaders have lost their moral compass. The polarisation of society through policies that have generated austerity, cruelty, poverty, division and lack of respect for the 'other' are now undermining that sense of community which we all need in order to feel that we 'belong'. This is expressed compellingly by Kate Smith, singer, music leader and entrepreneur, in her testimony *Reflections on Belonging and the Power of Creative Thinking*.

> *There is an illness in our society, a tragedy of modernity that is just beginning and is difficult to define, but deeply felt – I'm not unique in sensing it – it is the breakdown of community. Great forces are splintering us apart in order to feed perverse systems of value and power. (...)*

> *We don't have a concrete experience of community anymore – of what it means to share our home with people who are different from us. What have replaced our face-to-face interactions with people, what have supplanted our participation in politics – are the values of the market place. We have become fractured, independent, image obsessed consumers – our power lies in where we spend our money. And if we don't have money to spend, then we have no value to society, and hence no power. To multi-national corporations, the ideal citizen is a homogenised spender, and the law of the land is competition. In a society in which the power of unions is waning, and workers are switching to the gig economy, your individuality must become your brand. Our cities, our communities, our homes, our souls, are being colonised by corporate forces. There is less and less space for the true meaning of the public – space for all the people, in all their magnificent diversity.*

We are fragmented, lonely, stressed, anxious, powerless, depressed. We have turned in our concrete attachments to each other, in exchange for a false belief in 'homo economicus'.

What is the antidote? I don't propose we go back in time. But as we navigate this sea-change, we must be vigilant in promoting creativity, critical thinking, risk-taking, and collaboration. Everyone is inherently creative, but as the system tries to compress us into obedient online shoppers, the role of artists as torch-bearers for the human spirit is never more important. I have chosen to be an artist precisely because it helps keep me awake, curious, and questioning. The nature of art-making is to plumb the Unknown, seek out encounters with the Other, and communicate the human experience. Both in the art we create, as well as our way of creating, we embody the culture's conscience. Importantly, by creating with others and connecting through making, we become evangelists for the human spirit, recalling and awakening people to their own power as creative and worthwhile individuals, part of something bigger than themselves that yet needs and respects their contribution. To collaborate together in the creation of something new is a fundamentally democratic act. To take risks with each other, to experiment, and be allowed to fail, is to be seen and accepted despite and because of our faults, and to know we are not alone.

RESPONDING TO THE DIGITAL REVOLUTION

The source of Kate's motivation is explored further in Chapter 9. Her view of artists as 'torch-bearers for the human spirit' stands out as critical, not only in the divided political and social world but also in the new reality characterised by the digital revolution, in which the human aspect of 'being' can so easily be lost. This is captured well by Gil Teixera, a Portuguese musician writing from

Pittsburgh, Pennsylvania. Gil was the Founder of CEEMI, a Collaborative Experiential Electronic Musical Instrument that allows people to play together using tablets and smartphones. He is especially interested in the way in which music technology can be used as a means to enhance human interaction.

I feel that my life and work are literally mirroring what's happening in the world right now. Same crisis stage, same main underlying cause: the digital revolution. It may seem that the world has bigger fish to fry. Like far-right extremism and populism rising over much of the Western world, unprecedented high levels of depression, anxiety and stress among the younger generations, or the growing inequality in the distribution of wealth, but I see all of these and other problems of our time as different eruptions on the surface of the same subterranean and pervasive phenomenon.

The biggest challenge anyone faces in bringing awareness to the true dimensions and implications of this problem is epistemological. We have no objective distance whatsoever over it, no clear way of knowing how bad it is and how much worse it will become. We don't even have a comparable precedent in the history of mankind to hang on to. We're living it. We're all a bunch of 'digitots' lost in screens and apps, like boys with new toys, giving our first steps in a world that we can't possibly fully understand with the blind faith that all will be OK in the end. And it might, but it may also end up like the famous tobacco industry lawsuit. 50 years from now we might look back in horror to our digital infancy, to the countless hours we spend looking at screens, to the thoughtless way in which we allow them almost unrestricted access to our most personal data and surrender our attention to the huge corporations behind them.

We're overwhelmed. As the processing power of computers and smart devices keeps multiplying and the internet expanding beyond fathomable, we find it harder and harder to keep up. It's too much information, too fast, and on our end there's no Body 2.0 coming anytime soon. This is having a very negative impact on multiple aspects of our lives: first and foremost, in our physical and mental health. The digital is making us live more and more in the solitary confinement of our own brains. We don't use our bodies as much as we should, we don't spend enough time in face-to-face interactions and we are always 'on'. This is making us obese, depressed and burned out.

Gil, echoing Kate's commitment to the importance of 'creative collaborations', makes an equally convincing case for the place of the arts in young people's lives in this digital age. He pursues the source of his motivation in Chapter 5.

I firmly believe that the younger generations' engagement in creative projects has never been so important as at the present moment, because they are the ones dealing with the full scope of yet another paradox created by the digital age. At the same time that they have massive amounts of information readily accessible at their fingertips, they also have to face massive amounts of uncertainty when it comes to the road ahead. They are destined to enter a totally unscripted adulthood, with no near or distant echo in the history of mankind, and I'm afraid that we've been giving them the wrong tools to cope with that.

At least ever since my generation entered school the Western world has been utterly obsessed with providing its kids with hard skills in maths, sciences and engineering. And since the internet became a 'thing', that obsession has been particularly focused on selling us coding as the new lingua franca. Everything else, from arts and humanities to sports, has been labelled as either an after-school activity to be dropped as soon as college enters the horizon, or as a failed and unsuccessful life path. (...)

The main problem with this hard skills mindset is that it's completely blind to the fact that 'the times they are a-changing'. Human activity as we know it will be reshaped beyond recognition in a very short period of time and this will impact people's lives at the economic, social and psychological levels. Robots will soon replace us in all repetitive and non-cognitive tasks, and AI's will do the same for cognitive and non-repetitive tasks. Self-driving cars are just the tip of the iceberg of what's to come. Surgeons, engineers and other highly skilled and highly paid professionals will soon find themselves obsolete, not able to compete with the precision and knowledge level of machines. So what will be left for us humans to do? Ana Sofia Carvalho's views on this topic, from the European Group of Ethics in Science and New Technologies, as expressed in a recent interview with a Portuguese newspaper, totally resonate with mine. According to her, a part of the answer to this question lies necessarily in the so-called soft skills – like social and emotional intelligence and interpersonal communication – because "theoretically, at the mathematical and scientific levels, a machine can do better than a human, but at the relational level, the biggest achievement of the human being, no machine will ever be able to replace us".

The other and probably most meaningful part of that answer, and still quoting Ana Sofia, has to do with the realisation that "even more important than working on any kind of skills, is the urgent need to rethink people's core values. It's fundamental to prepare the younger generations for a future with less jobs, more robots, a need to redistribute wealth and more free time". This is where I believe that the engagement with the arts and creative processes in general can play a crucial role. There seems to be a weirdly significant overlap between the main traits usually associated with creative practice and the ones that can truly prepare our youth to face the epic challenges described above: creativity and imagination, resilience, critical thinking, collaboration, the ability to break down complex goals into small doable steps and playfulness. And just like any artist needs to face the empty page before a poem or a white canvas before a painting, young people today must do the same with the rest of their lives.

PREPARING FOR AN UNPREDICTABLE FUTURE

Each of these contributions brings a different, yet equally valid perspective to the urgent challenges confronting young people. Never have the challenges been greater, and never has it been more important for those organisations responsible for students and emerging artists to engage seriously with their concerns in order to prepare them for what might well be an unpredictable future. One person who empathises with the dilemmas, uncertainties and seeming disconnectedness of young people is Rick Holland, a writer and tutor at the Guildhall School. In his testimony he raises several germane questions drawn from his own experience as a perceived 'outsider'.

How many young people, for many reasons feel (…) disconnected or disenfranchised in some way from social groupings, society, their cultures? Young people thirst for culture that represents them, to celebrate being alive and to help assuage life's difficulties, and if they cannot find that culture, they make it. My deepest motivation is the honouring of authentic culture, especially when it is marginalised or judged. I don't pretend to link my experience to other forms of disenfranchisement, but I do translate a sensitivity from my own experience to that of other human beings.

I turned to creative writing initially as an escape, writing short stories that I still remember now, poignant and symbolic and not so different from the methods of writing I have explored in adulthood. Having started this at a very young age I developed a way of engaging with the world, of describing it, that I could spend a great length of time in. It championed the inner world of experience, it enjoyed the sensations of language use beyond rhetoric and formal knowledge. It started from a place of instinctive collecting and celebrated its own music. I think many writers and creatively minded people will have a similar account, particularly those living in a world in which it was possible to spend a lot of time alone. This was a common experience for people of my generation, with working parents, no mobile phones or computers, and in my case a lot of childhood spent away from home.

In living this mode every day, a parallel live naming of the world and experience within it developed through my teens and twenties. A voice emerged in my daily practice of poetically describing what I saw, to sit alongside and challenge the conventional narratives around in the consumer blur of a conservative nation exploring a confident but hollow material individualism. My live naming was symbolic and often music led, and continued to drink up cultures and contexts by listening very closely. The resistance of authority continued, part of a battle to keep faith in a way of being that has been hard fought for in the face of societal pressures. It is fair to say that in this period of my life, the disconnects in personal and political identity manifested themselves in a prolonged period of poor mental health. In hindsight, it is really no surprise, but stigma was rife in such matters, and we have started to make important strides in those areas. Again, I don't like to present this as identity, preferring to look forwards, but it is a key factor of experience of youth that links me emphatically with young people today.

Rick is very honest about how he tried to make sense of a complex, dislocated childhood through harnessing his deeply felt creative energy and imagination – that's what fed his early life as a writer and a musician, as is discussed further in Chapter 5. This lived understanding has enabled him to relate to those many young artists who are yearning to put their own stamp on what feels to them a pretty hostile world.

I believe we are in a stage of huge transition, and that like any huge transition there have been plenty of false starts. The open source nature of the internet in development has been swallowed by markets and widespread normalisation of cultures and people, and the brave new world of connectivity has temporarily rendered us dangerously isolated and atomised.

'Swallowed by markets' perhaps sums up the state of the world at the moment, and the need for strongly formulated counters to the bland destruction of culture has never been more pressing.

A younger generation grows up seeing a form of politics at play that bears no resemblance to their perceptions of life, and political concerns are replaced by economic survival and narratives of competition and danger. This is the central characteristic of the neoliberal world, encouraging individualism and suggesting a value system based on money and sales, not quality of relation to other human beings based on shared value sets that promote our best interests.

We need to risk naivety. The task is huge. The work of young people, as ever, reminds us how far we have let them down. Age brings a growing pragmatism in many ways, but it also shuts off the emitting hub, the real being, when it is swallowed by too much context, and mature people commonly make the mistake of enforcing the system they have fought for a place within. I wonder how many young people feel muted. Figures suggest that it is a great many, with pathologies of anxiety and depression surging.

'What does 'now' feel like?' could be the most important question we can ask. Forget for a minute (a long minute) the markers of funding and assessment, or at least put them where they belong, in service of real and lived experience and a commitment to progress. In very simple terms, I feel that promoting this question in my own work and in others is my response to the world as it is. My current work is hand-made and very slow in production. It involves slow relationships with other creative humans, a printer primarily at the moment, and a deliberate reduction of attention.

These extracts serve as a clarion call for action. They are drawn from the whole spectrum of 'youth voice', ranging from 16 to 40 years of age, and they demonstrate a keen social and political awareness. No one is happy with the status quo and there are very good reasons to encourage these young people to respond to the injustices of the world through exercising their creativity and imagination. And that's exactly what they're doing in their different ways as will be seen throughout *Young Artists Speak Out.*

5

THE ARTS: IDENTITY AND BELONGING

A CASE FOR ENGAGING IN CREATIVITY AND THE ARTS

This chapter seeks to demonstrate how one's search for identity and sense of belonging can be enhanced through engaging in the arts. In whatever social context we find ourselves, making and performing art can unlock our creative voice, open new doors, extend our personal boundaries and provide opportunities for us to understand who we are. The arts can be a source of inspiration, a celebration of the human spirit and can enhance the quality and meaning of our lives. The bold inventiveness of the arts, their ability to challenge our assumptions and help us see ourselves, others and the world through a different lens, must never be allowed to atrophy due to competing economies fighting to survive. (See Renshaw, 2013, p.4)

No government can afford to ignore the rich artistic, creative, emotional and spiritual benefits gained from actively engaging in the arts. People's lives can be transformed through participating in the arts – by strengthening their self-esteem, self-respect and sense of identity, by working together and developing a feeling of belonging, by seeking a measure of connectedness and coherence through different arts experiences. One of the main threads throughout *Young Artists Speak Out* shows how creative collaborative processes can enable any person, young or old, to build up a strong sense of who they are by empowering them to believe in themselves and take responsibility for their own lives and for those of others.

Two recent reports in England provide evidence of the important link between engaging in the arts and strengthening a person's sense of identity and belonging. The Durham Commission on Creativity and Education (2019), discussed in Chapter 4, explored the place that creativity can play in the development of individual and collective identity, mobility and wellbeing. For example, it states that:

> *The value of creativity in promoting social engagement, community identity and cohesion is strongly associated with the concept of creative placemaking, in which civically engaged individuals come together to create shared public spaces that encourage engagement, wellbeing, and a locally focused quality of experience in their communities. (p.30)*

From its research, the Commission concludes that:

> *Creativity and creative thinking can help young people to develop the imagination and empathy to care for each other and their communities. Young citizens should be able to recognise needs and solve problems, understanding the strengths that grow from diversity and shaping strong communities that are formed from many points of view. (ibid., p.31)*

In the Commission's discussion of wellbeing it emphasises that:

> *Creativity can shape a holistic, life-long approach to health and wellbeing. Creative activities can be shared*

and are a means of self-realisation; they can help with physical fitness and emotional resilience and can contribute to needs at different ends of the age-scale – we now see young people in primary schools struggling with mental health and loneliness. The rise of technology has also been attributed to poorer mental health, although it brings with it opportunities for creative expression which itself drives wellbeing. (ibid., p.39)

The second seminal report, *The Sound of the Next Generation*, produced by Youth Music and Ipsos MORI (2019), comprised a comprehensive review of children and young people's relationship with music[10]. As in the case of the Durham Commission, the wellbeing of young people was seen to be of growing concern and the Youth Music report provides strong evidence that engaging in creative collaborative music-making is good for a person's mental health. For example:

Research shows that music has a positive impact on wellbeing. It enables young people to connect with their peers, their community, their family and their roots. Making music as a group physically brings people together, encouraging teamwork, empathy and social bonding. It makes a positive contribution to young people's subjective wellbeing – a positive state of mind where they feel good about their life, and its constituent parts (such as their relationships with others and how they see themselves). Subjective wellbeing can be assessed by measuring mental states including anxiety, happiness, life satisfaction, meaning, sadness, stress and worthwhileness. (p.16)

One crucial point here is that 'making music', creating music that responds to mood, feelings and states of being, has a more

---

[10] Youth Music and Ipsos MORI (2019). *The Sound of the Next Generation.*

significant impact on the wellbeing of young people than just listening to it:

> *Research suggests that the creative process of making music has a deeper and more profound impact than listening to it. The young people we spoke to substantiated this, seeing music-making as a vital part of their lives and something which made them feel worthwhile. (ibid., p.16)*

Another vital conclusion was that those young people engaged with making music, especially in a collaborative context, were projecting into the future in a more positive way than many of those not involved with music-making.

> *The experiences of young people included in our study align with the wider evidence – that listening to and playing music is a vital way of regulating and articulating emotions, developing social bonds and feeling more in control of life. Young people are using music as a resource to draw on, a coping mechanism to support their personal wellbeing. They're doing this creatively, strategically and – often independently. There's an opportunity therefore for schools, charities and arts organisations to support young people to use music in this way. To re-imagine the purpose of music and music education for social and wellbeing outcomes. And in doing so, make it more inclusive and impactful. (ibid., p.18)*

THE SEARCH FOR MEANING AND CONNECTEDNESS

In this section, four young creatives illustrate their very individual responses to how engaging in the arts brings meaning and a sense of connectedness into their lives – a connection to different realities. First, the contrasting voices of two members of the Barbican Young Poets, a poetry workshop and community for young writers led by the poet and performer Jacob Sam-La Rose and supported by the Barbican Centre in London: Michelle Tiwo and Bella Cox.

BLM (Black Lives Matter)
by Michelle Tiwo, Barbican Young poet

Anger is Black because murder stole all the red
while ignorance was too busy leaving brown bodies lying
till blue for the mo(u)rning 'cause ignorance stay green
bout angers power and its colour
don't like the way it boils over
or how it smells fearless – Ready

to paint the cities walls
or burn them down
or die trying.

Neither birthplace nor genetics, still home
by Bella Cox, Barbican Young Poet

After Sumia Jaama's 'Before Leaving'

Any phone number beginning +254 / is a trip wire / stretched across your heartbeat / you jolt to hear the phone ring loud and long in your hand / the map of the world pulls slowly / in and out of focus / you do not answer / when breath returns / you call back to hear the voicemail greeting playing on loop / samahani, mteja wa nambari uliopiga, hapatikani kwa sasa / in the kitchen you search for matoke and lost accents / but find only crumpets and snow on the window sill / when your new friends call / their phone numbers are granted local status 0 / no additions needed for belonging / you answer on the second ring / English can sound so curt and stiff / you say asante sana / forget they do not know this tongue on you / all the mangoes here have lost their sweetness / a man on the street points at the African pendant on your cream neck / asks if you're from there / ndiyo sounds old in your mouth / the way truths can gather dust when neglected / he tells you of a home you do not share / you try to find common ground in the red earth he describes / thankful this man did not assume tourist / sometimes in bed / you dial numbers you know will go to voicemail / and lull yourself into dreams / birds of paradise rising

The Delphic maxim, 'Know Thyself', has been much debated since Socrates and the Greeks, and of course it is as pertinent today as it was so many years ago. But this search for self-knowledge, for coming to know who one is, has become a burning issue in the complex contemporary world of LGBTQ+, in which questions of gender, race and identity assume over-riding importance. The theme, 'What it means to be me', is explored with great honesty by Abbi Asante in her testimony written towards the end of her 3rd Year on the BA course in Performance and Creative Enterprise at the Guildhall School. Abbi is a powerful singer who through her search for 'being herself' hopes to inspire and empower others on similar journeys. What stands out in her testimony is her uncompromising honesty about who she is and how she strives to be herself through her music. Her singing is her raison d'être. Her voice and her lyrics lie at the heart of her identity. Abbi's testimony is both a personal and political statement.

The same can be said about the testimony by Lauren Saunders, a visual artist working in Hull. Lauren sees the connection between art, identity and belonging very clearly. For her as an artist, the synergy between her inner creative voice and the challenges confronting the outside world is her lifeline. In fact, this dynamic symbiotic relationship between the inner and the outer lies at the core of what it is to be an artist who is socially engaged. Inner creative energy always needs to be nurtured but then put to the service of others, connecting and responding to their needs. This is not seen as an act of altruism, but one of moral necessity.

———o———

Testimony by Abbi Ashanti, singer

What it means to be me: an androgynous, black, dark-skinned, queer, woman in the music industry

There was a time in my life. When I first started out. When I had to make some decisions. When I came out I was wearing tuxedos, my hair was nappy as fuck and people used to talk so much shit. I mean really! To the point where I was like 'I need to change'.

Like seriously I just really wanted to say to everybody out here, honestly I know, I know.

When you're doing something you feel convicted in it, maybe nobody has walked down that road. You have mentors and idols but nobody is doing the shit you're trying to do. Just know that you are going to inspire so many people by embracing what makes you unique, even if it makes other uncomfortable. Stay with it, stay with it. I just want y'all to know that there was a moment in my life where I said: 'Imma go Crazy on these Niggas!"

(Janelle Monáe - AFROPunk Festival 2016)

I stood in the front row of the AFROPunk festival in Brooklyn, New York, and let those words wash over me. A Black face amongst a sea full of Black faces all holding their blackness close but wearing their identities differently. It was in that moment I realised I had to reclaim myself and my identity, not only for my sake but for others.

I didn't know who I was, only what the world expected me to be and I was not okay with that. We were all not okay with that. The reason for the AFROPunk festival is for black people and their allies to have a sense of freedom and be their fully dimensional selves.

Janelle Monáe gave us this speech before she came out as the Pansexual, Queer icon people see today. She had some things she needed to work out before she felt comfortable coming into that queer spotlight and so did I. This is my story.

> *To be white is to be human; to be white is universal. I only know this because I am not.*
> (Reni Eddo-Lodge, 2017, p. xvii)

I identify as a black.
I identify as a woman.
I identify as bisexual.
I identify as queer.

In a world such as mine, where I am a minority almost everywhere I go, representation in the media is very important for me. I have to do some purposeful looking before I can see myself beyond my bedroom mirror and in the wider world.

Until most recently there weren't any black, queer, dark skinned, female leads on network television. Even then there was only one with mainstream success. Annalise Keating (portrayed by Viola Davis) on 'How To Get Away With Murder' was the first time I *ever* felt like I saw myself represented on TV and that character wasn't aired until late 2014.

Here's a blog post I made in 2015 about Viola's impact on me:

> *If you know me well, you know how much I love and adore and absolutely admire actress Viola Davis (and even saying that is an understatement lol).*
> *Well (clears throat) her presence in 'mainstream' media has really made me feel... **normal**.*

*I cried when I watched the first episode of 'How To Get Away With Murder'. Because I finally saw a black **dark skin** woman play a role with a purpose, no sassiness, no maid, no slave, no crook, no 'yes suh or yes ma'am', but a confident woman, sure of who she is, just a **whole person** imperfections and all!*

Gave me hope, changed the game for me, made my features feel less alien. I see in her the things that I usually don't like about myself, things that society deem as unattractive (until the Kardashians do it smh -__-) like her shapely figure, full lips, dark skin and broad nose, broad shoulders, ooo and her 'deep' voice!

All things I've personally been very conscious about, she has made it feel alright, normal, human. Representation is important!!

*I'm a 19-year-old, imagine how our young girls feel and have them to grow up feeling inferior, having them only view themselves as a background character. One black/POC background character in the whole of a production is **not** diversity.*

What Viola is doing now, I want to do also.

But even still, throughout Hollywood and the world, it feels as though I'm only seeing one version of me, one version of a black woman. The lighter skinned, slim, more feminine Halle Berry's, Beyoncé's, and Thandie Newton's still dominate our on-screen narratives. And when you do have the few dark skin black women, their roles were always limited to stereotypes: the non-sexual, the strong black woman, motherly, or sassy types. All of which I recognise and are true to some, but don't completely identify with. To list a few:

Viola Davis in *Doubt*
Octavia Spencer in *The Help*
Gabourey Sidibe in *Precious*
Whoopi Goldberg in *Ghost*

Whoopi Goldberg started off in Hollywood as a force to be reckoned with. She was funny, but not at her own expense in *Jumpin' Jack Flash* (1986). She was a stand-up comedian and social commentator in her one woman show Direct from Broadway (1985). She was a rugged cop in *Fatal Beauty* (1987), and a lovable burglar in the movie *Burglar* (1987). But she didn't really hit it big and win a Grammy until she became the **sassy** (tick one), **crook/criminal** (tick two) and **secondary character** (tick three) in the movie *Ghost* (1990).

Let me not forget to mention that black pain sells. We've seen all those movies about the struggles of the civil rights movement, the struggles of slavery, the struggles of the ghetto, the struggles of modern-day slavery (incarceration and police brutality). But we are more than our struggles and that is something I want to get across to the world.

> *Is that what it takes to create a sympathetic black lead*
> *character? I could imagine the board meeting.*
> *She has to be obese!*
> *She has to be super poor.*
> *She has to be illiterate!*
> *She has to have an abusive mother who molests her.*
> *She has to be a rape victim of her **father**!*
> *She has to be teenage and pregnant.*
> *She has to be HIV positive.*
> *She has to have a baby with Down's syndrome!*
> *Now we care about this character...*
> (Issa Rae, 2015, pp.38-39)

Right now there's a shift happening where black folk are taking charge of their narrative and are writing their own stories. I aim to be a part of that shift.

Shonda Rhimes is a screenwriter and producer who has created her own TV empire ShondaLand by writing critically acclaimed shows such as *Grey's Anatomy*, *Scandal* and *How To Get Away With Murder*. All these shows star and/or feature women and people of colour, and they are always written with more than their race in mind. This makes them more relatable to across the spectrum, and more realistic.

Issa Rae is a screenwriter and producer who made the web series (now TV show), *The Misadventures of an Awkward Black Girl*. Where she comments on and makes jokes about stuff like workplace drama, love life, family life etc. Just the normal everyday things which we barely see black folk to be a part of in the media. Issa continues to support other upcoming screenwriters by allowing submissions for short films and web series to feature on her YouTube channel.

Lena Waithe wrote and portrayed a young black lesbian coming out to her family for an episode on the Netflix show *Master of None*. It was the first time I saw a queer black woman come out to her family on TV. She won an Emmy for that episode and it warmed my heart to see a masculine-of-centre black woman, wearing a suit, accepting an Emmy award, and thanking her girlfriend. Inspiring to say the least!

Lena urges young queer people to come out and be themselves so to humanise our community and lessen the stigma.

I hope this acceptance of us and our stories isn't just a phase.
And there's more work to be done.
That's where I come in.

[…] My wants and needs are simple
make music that moves and also has a principle.
It has to have intention,
that's why I'm obliged to mention
that I am still black
no matter if you colour blind me
it won't erase the complexity
of what I grew up dealing with
the heart aches and the sword-tongued kids,
who before WAKANDA was a thing
spoke down to the girl with extra melanin.

Before Janelle said 'highly melanated'
I was afraid to stand in my grace
it's amazing.

I hope my blackness is not a trend,
I hope the love never ends.
In my world black is the new black
and that is that because there's no other fact.
It is what it is.
I once dreamed of having lighter skinned kids
just so they wouldn't go through the shit that I did."
(Abbi Asante, Somehow I Still Love, March 2018)

Caring for myself is not self-indulgence, it is an act of self-
preservation and that is an act of political warfare.
(Audre Lourde, 2017)

Sometimes in order to move forward, we must take a step back; understand the past, understand our roots and where we've come from. I took the years of 2017 and 2018 to do that. Reclaiming the identity I had before I became, and tried to be as monolithic and easily digestible as possible.

I called it Abbi Academy and for a few weeks I revisited all the things outside my musical craft that made me happy. I began playing football again, going on spontaneous runs, boxing and sketching. In doing that, I gave myself permission just to *be*, and that's all I could have asked for.

In a world where being myself is a political statement, I needed to find another outlet that wasn't songwriting, something that didn't make my pain tangible but instead allowed that energy to be let out into the universe. I felt a freedom I hadn't felt. And that bled into my work; my songwriting became less burdened with the tension I soak from the world. And within that freedom I was able to be honest with myself, I was able to come out to myself and state that I am queer.

> *"Being born gay, black and female is not a revolutionary act, but being proud to be a gay, black female is."*
> (Lena Waithe)

I plan on being myself through my music more than ever. Because I can't help it. Because it's a political statement. Because it will make others feel less alone. And I hope more than anything to inspire and empower others along the way.

> *Art is my weapon in the ongoing battle against indifference and inaction.*
> (Harmonia Rosales)

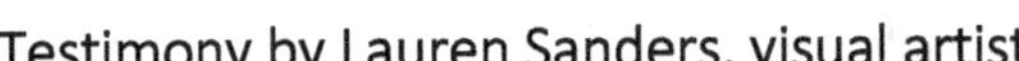

Testimony by Lauren Sanders, visual artist

My name is Lauren Saunders, and I am an emerging visual artist living in the current UK City of Culture, Hull. I'm not from Hull originally though. I grew up in North London and moved 'oop nuurth' in 2012 after completing a Foundation Degree. I'm also a recent graduate of one of the oldest art schools in the UK, Hull School of Art and Design after topping-up with a BA (Hons). Alongside developing my own creative practice at this early stage of my career, I work in the NHS promoting good mental health and meaningful mental health recovery.

But what does any of that tell you, I wonder? As I'm writing I'm also wondering where to start when thinking about how I feel about the world. Do I begin with what I feel affects me as a young person? An artist? A woman? A British citizen? Do I start with issues that concern me locally? Or nationally? Or globally? Maybe I could kill two birds with one stone here. I look at the world around me and my place in it, and I can see where I come from privilege, but also where I face adversity. You need to know where I come from, understand the things I encounter, see the lots I've been allocated – so you can understand why I feel so passionately about the things that matter to me.

I am a young, white British female. I was born into a loving family who have always allowed me to make my own choices. I have the best mum anyone could ask for. I had a good education, so I can read and write, and I have a degree in a subject I freely chose and passionately enjoy. I have access to free healthcare via the NHS and access to electricity, water and state welfare. I am able to work, and I have a meaningful permanent job working under a boss who appreciates me and within an amazing team. I am able to start up my own creative practice. I am entitled to vote. As a woman, I can choose what to do with my life and my body, and have free access to contraception. I earn enough to keep a roof over my head and food on my plate. I have clean clothes and am clean. I have no personal debt. I have all the things I need to survive and contribute to a functioning society. I have a loving long-term boyfriend and a beautiful cat. We are all physically healthy and mobile. I feel loved and appreciated by those around me. I am able to pursue my own interests at will. I have a talent for art, which I am recognised for. England has an Arts Council (alongside other lots of money dedicated to the arts) that could fund some of the projects I hope to do. I have an awful lot of privilege and opportunity compared to most people in the world, to which I feel humbled and grateful.

I am working class. My family wasn't rich enough to send me to a school which would guarantee me respect, connections and security in later life. I was encouraged by the state education system to pursue anything but the Arts. I didn't fit in at the prestigious Arts school I first got into, so I felt I had no choice but to leave. I have no assets, no savings and I am unable to secure a mortgage, let alone own my own home. I cannot pursue my dream of owning a self-build sustainable 'tiny home' in the woods somewhere because I do not own any land, and even if I did, I'd probably be stopped by UK planning permissions. I get ridiculed because I care for the environment and ethical sustainability, and for the choices I make to reduce my footprint. I have genuinely lost count of how much I owe in student loans. I rent a tiny little flat in one of the UKs most economically deprived areas. Because I scrimp and live on the cheap in an attempt to do everything I can to avoid personal debt or environmental waste, I am seen as a bit of an oddball/scrooge by others. Because I rent, I am unable to run an arts business from home. The North does not have the opportunity or wealth the South does. I could never afford to move back into my hometown of London. I have to turn down creative or meaningful personal opportunities, or else struggle like hell, because I cannot afford to take a break from work to focus fully on something else.

The NHS, the organisation I am proud to work for, faces greater and greater cuts as the demand for need increases, meaning the workforce and I feel the pressure to do more for less. I feel as if my vote doesn't matter in the country I live in. I voted to Remain in the Brexit vote, yet I will still lose out to important EU Arts funding (amongst a million other things). I would love to move to the Netherlands, but I do not have the resources, or possibly soon, the right, to do so. I feel as if the current government has no interest in the greater good. I see greater levels of homelessness, poverty and disadvantage than I've ever noticed.

I come from a 'broken'/non-traditional family. I have suffered poor mental health since about 6 years old. I have tried to kill myself on a number of occasions in the past. And then get labelled an 'attention seeker' if I talk about it. I experience disabling episodes which can stop me from living fully. I take medication for it that some months I struggle to afford. I get laughed at for pursuing alternatives. I feel unable to work full-time again because I worry for my mental wellbeing. I get questioned about why I'm not married to my boyfriend and have no kids with him. And I get looks of shock when I say that I'm not interested in either. I don't fit the modern Western concept of beauty. I feel an internal struggle about it too because I both don't care about it, and do. I have been bullied since childhood, primarily because of my appearance. The media is constantly telling me what to look like, what to feel, what to buy, how to vote and how to think. I feel trapped by an apparent practical and mental reliance on the internet, especially on social media (even though I know it's not a true representation of others). I live in a society where the Arts are not valued (and therefore, my skills and offerings are not as valued as they should be). As an artist, I always get asked why I don't just settle for a 'proper' job. I am too young to have enough confidence, experience or to be taken seriously, but too old to be offered 'springboard' opportunities. I cannot afford my own studio space to make work.

I genuinely hope that didn't sound like one big whinge (it felt like one writing it!). I don't tend to complain too much in real life, but these are just some of the things that I feel have shaped, are shaping and will continue to shape my life. I am grateful for the great things I have, of course I am. But when you acknowledge that you are denied the simple things you want to achieve because you don't have the right background, appearance, connections and/or because you have a disability, it's near impossible not to feel angry. I'm sure most people can relate to this feeling, whether they share my adversities or experience others (e.g. race, cultural expectations, tragedies). I'm also sure you've noticed a common thread woven within them all: 'Justice'

– or rather, the lack of it. I recognise that stuff happens that we cannot control (e.g. illness, natural disasters), but most of the things that I find wrong with the world on both a general and personal level have to do with human greed, nepotism, control, self-serving attitudes and ignorances. It's frustrating because these injustices which affect me and many, many others are within human control.

I've been told before that I've chosen to make life harder for myself because I want to pursue my art ("You're so smart – you could have been a Doctor or a Lawyer!"). Aye, ta for that observation. Why do I 'make' then, if it's so hard to make a living off it? It's quite a challenge to pin down exactly 'why'. It's a lot of things I think, both things I'm conscious of and things I'm not.

Without a shadow of a doubt, engaging with the arts and creativity can make a qualitative difference to a young person's life. I say this with absolute conviction because it has done to mine. Allow me to explain...

I notice that art-making allows me to explore, develop and actualise my personal values as a textbook INFJ type personality: Creativity, Compassion/Love, Personal Growth, Achievement and Fulfilment, Making a Difference and Personal Wellbeing.

My values are important to me as they keep me feeling mentally, emotionally and spiritually well as I navigate the world; 'Making' is a vehicle in which I can express my core being, a way to articulate myself and not only to identify my position in relation to other things or people, but also to challenge the injustices I see in the world. It is known that the more you can do to 'feed' these values, the happier you will be; with this in mind, I think it becomes clear why I am so passionate about it. It makes me happy!

Art has a tendency to allow you to develop a heightened sense of self-awareness – by looking outward, you learn an awful lot about what is inward. And when you look inward, you learn an awful lot about what is underneath. Then by acknowledging what is underneath, you can better understand how you feel or interpret things when looking outward. Art and visual language helps me to understand myself by developing a dialogue between the part of me that cares about 'out there' and the part of me that needs to think about 'me'. Who am I? What do I find important? What can I do about it? Why do I make? Who is it for? I have also found that art is not only a vehicle for self-discovery, but can also become a very big part of someone's identity in itself. What is identity? What does it mean to be an artist? Why art? Art, and the processes that lie beyond the paint, so to speak (such as critical thinking, reflection, research and development), becomes a practical tool with which to explore the concept of 'me'. This can be so useful especially for young people, who often are still developing a sense of identity.

The question of identity has a lot to do with the concept of belonging. How your ideals, values, motivations as in an individual align with others? Stereotypically, artists are these odd-ball dreamers who talk of abstract ideas, dress and behave strangely and create all manner of bizarre things at unsociable hours. Artists are not all like that, obviously, but there is a grain of truth to that stereotype; by nature of their pursuits, creatives do see things a bit differently to 'normal people in society'. Creatives **do** question things, experiment and problem-solve, meaning that yes, sometimes the boat is rocked. The point I'm trying to make is that artists and creators can be on the fringes of society because of how they interact with the world. As an artist, I love being around other artists. Like, seriously. If I seriously contemplated with my dad (a proper football-mad 'bloke') about the character of that red line and its relationship with that melancholy shape and if a Marxist squirrel was to sit on the painting would it think that bit there was a bit of grass because of the technical qualities of that area (or other such nonsense), he would give me a funny look, laugh, and then do anything to change the subject. In contrast, I can think about 11 people within my direct art community that would critically entertain the concept before inevitably allowing the conversation to blossom into something bigger and more meaningful. Knowing I am an artist, knowing that Art is a big part of my identity, allows me to seek out others who share similar perspectives. Art gives me a sense of belonging.

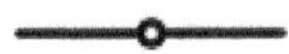

THE SYNERGY BETWEEN THE INNER AND THE OUTER

The synergy between the inner and the outer is picked up by Jana Thiel, an American musician who at the time of writing was working at the International School in Helsinki, where she taught children with behavioural and learning difficulties. She was also a creative music leader in her very active church community, where they make new music together and write songs in Finnish and English. Jana reflects on where authentic creativity is born in her very succinct testimony, *Collision Point*.

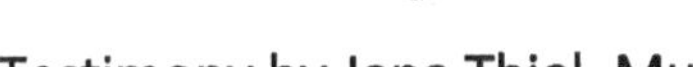

Testimony by Jana Thiel, Musician

Collision Point

In
Out
Inhale
Exhale
Internal
External
Expiration
Inspiration
External
Internal
Out
In

Breathing is fundamental to living. But to breathe requires a giving and receiving. There's an exchange of chemicals and a transference which provides the required elements for life to exist. The practice of breathing can be seen as the connection between the internal and external worlds. You receive something from the outside to exchange within yourself and then release an exchanged element into the atmosphere. This place of meeting in the body is the blood cells, exchanging oxygen and carbon dioxide as it passes through the lungs and heart to make this vital life exchange. Without this collision and exchange there is not life. The collision within the body is a physical representation of the collision of internal and external we experience in other areas of life and being. This is the interesting place of existence. It's where, body, mind, spirit, and heart all combine into the soul. It is the place that is the most painful to explore. It is the place that is the hardest to identify. Collision and exchange can be ugly, microscopic, and painful. Moments that are difficult to define and explore. Moments we like to avoid. Moments we like to ignore. But without these moments you only offer half of yourself to the world. Without allowing yourself to fully experience them, you cannot fully experience life. Going through the motions of existence is not fully living. To be a whole being requires an exploration of places where you feel most vulnerable. You are not what you absorb. You are not what you give. Who you are is hidden in that place where these elements of internal and external collide and exchange. The place that no one except you can fully experience. Where you, the true you, brings something new into existence — where authentic creativity is born.

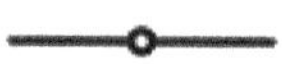

This reciprocal relationship, the interconnectedness between the inner and the outer, lies at the heart of any reflective artist. It is integral to the process of coming to know oneself as a person and as an artist – a continuous search for meaning, an honest understanding of one's engagement with the world and a sensitive awareness of the possibilities that might lie ahead. This is explored in a very personal way by Gil Teixera, the Portuguese musician who explores his attitude to the digital revolution in Chapter 4. In the first part of his testimony he responds to the fundamental questions 'why do you do what you do?', 'what is the source of your motivation?' and 'what are your values?'

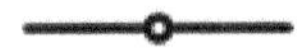

Testimony by Gil Teixera, Musician

I couldn't think of a more interesting moment to be asked these questions than the present one. I'm currently standing at the blurry peak of a massive paradigm shift that affects all vectors of my life, struggling to focus on a new and clear path. Some people say that this is just what happens when one is about to turn 40 - the so-called midlife crisis. I say that my current state is a direct consequence of a series of concrete events and not of how many springs I have lived so far. Yet, almost annoyingly so, they do seem to coincide in my case.

Looking back at my recent past, I can easily pinpoint the main triggers for my current crisis, or at least the ones that I'm aware of. I'll start with the one that shook me to the core: in October 2016 I became a father. All of a sudden there was a part of me that was outside of me, staring back at me, demanding time and attention, refusing to fit my plans and my work schedule. A part of me that escaped my illusion of control: a part of me that was not me. For the first time in my life I felt forced to step out of my own ego and truly tune in to someone else's needs.

This might sound strange coming from an artist engaged for most of his life in collaborative community projects, but when it comes to the driving force of my artistic practice so far, along with Amalia, my daughter, a deep suspicion was born. How much of my motivation to engage others in creative projects stemmed out of genuine empathy and how much was just the satisfaction of an egotistical need? How much of the process and outcome of those projects was based on collaboration versus manipulation?

This suspicion went even further back in time to my formative years and early 20s, a period of my life when I was basically shooting in all directions, expanding my skill set and interests as a 21st century Renaissance man. Academically speaking I went from pure physics to philosophy, German and classical guitar. As an artist I went from playing repertoire on my classical guitar, to composing and playing in a post rock band, writing short stories in local press, amateur film making and VJing, electronic music production, coding, etc. I was mostly focused on being unfocused and never satisfied, always striving for more, but why did I invest so much time and energy expanding my skills in so many directions? Was I genuinely interested in all of them or was I simply trying too hard to get attention? Or was my perfectionist self, afraid of not ever being good enough at something if I dared to dedicate myself entirely to just one of them?

For the last five years I actually dared to tackle this last question, by dedicating myself almost exclusively to the exploration of the intersection between music, people and digital technology: a path that eventually led me to the remaining triggers of my paradigm shift. This path began at the Guildhall School of Music & Drama in London during my Master's in Music Leadership. It's hard to describe what the course was about, but its main threads at the time were cross-artistic and cross-cultural collaboration and community-based creative projects. In hindsight I would describe it now as my very own trip to Neverland, with all the appeals and dangers that one immediately associates with it. Never before or after the course did I manage to be engaged in so many and so diverse artistic collaborations and projects that would just fall on my lap with no need for admin, promotion or networking. Every artist's dream for sure, with the obvious downside that one can't stay in Neverland forever. Another aspect of the course that was simultaneously its best and worst quality was the fact that anyone who went through it was pushed so far out of their comfort zone to find their own artistic voice, that they either got out of it (delete on) a new, strong and clear artistic path or were lost forever in a pool of infinite possibilities. My story is particularly interesting in this respect because I ended up in both scenarios.

As part of my final project for the course I started working on CEEMI, a Collaborative Experiential Electronic Musical Instrument that allowed people to play music together using tablets and smartphones. I truly believed that the digital revolution would provide me with the missing link between my chosen art form and those around me, a way to bring people in with no prior musical training to a collective musical experience that was neither scary nor patronising. And it did, but as time moved forward I got more and more sucked into the development of the tool itself, putting every other side of my artistic life on hold, believing that CEEMI would soon feel complete. It never did. It never will. There's always one more important feature, one more bug, one more request. The law of conservation of energy doesn't seem to apply to the digital realm. It sucks your energy and never gives it back to you in any form. On the other hand, Murphy's Laws seem to apply to it times a million, as if on steroids. Even when nothing could go wrong, it still went wrong. I can't recall how many times things went terribly wrong with CEEMI in workshop settings. I do recall however and very vividly the resulting high levels of stress, frustration and embarrassment. I feel burned out by the whole process and ready to move on.

This is where I stand right now. Orphan of a medium and of an inner driving force to my artistic creation. The biggest irony is that precisely five years ago in London, at the peak of my passion for the digital, a random guy in a random party tried to save me all this trouble by telling me precisely where that path would lead me and what was wrong with it. He was an artist himself. Puppetry was his medium. As I babbled about all the amazing possibilities inherent to the musical exploration of touch devices, coding, etc, he listened with this weirdly patronising look in his face. When I finally gave him the space to talk, he told me: "Gil, I've been there, done that. Max MSP, SuperCollider, touch devices, Arduinos, sensors, you name it. Do you know why I do puppetry now? Because the digital is only infinite at the surface, deep down it is finite by definition – it's all a stream of zeros and ones. Our bodies and any other physical material however are truly infinite and continuous, and that's why there's no algorithm in the world that will ever be able to give me the same joy and fulfilment than a piece of wood being carved into a puppet". I was not ready to listen. He was absolutely right.

Looking ahead into my foggy horizon I would just like to add that I may not know yet what is my puppet, my new medium, nor what will drive me to work on it, but I have faith in my core guiding values showing me the way because they have remained constant throughout all my previous redefining moments and relevant in all stops of both my artistic and life paths. The first one is resonance. There's something very powerful and beautiful in the notion of two bodies vibrating effortlessly in the same frequency. It's the ultimate win/win situation. That's why I know that whatever I do next it will need to resonate with me and with those around me. It will also necessarily happen in between: in between disciplines, mediums, tools and people. The only thing that my scattered path made me really good at is making connections. I'm an expert in the space between all the fields where I'm an amateur. And finally there's Sankofa, probably the most relevant in my current situation. Sankofa is not a word, it's an adinkra symbol from Ghana. It's represented by a bird with its head turned backwards while its feet face forward carrying a precious egg in its mouth. It's usually associated with the proverb "It is not wrong to go back for that which you have forgotten". As I let go of the development of CEEMI and reflect on my path to write these words, I can finally feel my head turning.

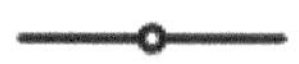

Again, what is so striking about Gil's reflections is his honesty as he appraises where he is at in his personal and professional life at the moment. His commitment to resonance and the importance of interconnectedness will undoubtedly remain at the forefront of what he does, but his earlier search for what drives him raises major dilemmas that confront many artists as they try to disentangle why they engage in 'collaborative community projects'. Does this stem from 'genuine empathy' or 'egotistical need'? How far are process and outcome based on 'collaboration' or 'manipulation'? These pertinent questions need to be asked by any artist who is socially engaged, but they are very challenging and easily side-stepped. Gil shows us a way forward.

As does Rick Holland, the Guildhall PACE tutor, who was writing at the end of Chapter 4. In this part of Rick's testimony his reflections about identity and feeling an 'Outsider' must resonate with many young people today. What he has to say offers a challenge to anyone trying to make sense of who they are – coming to terms with their past, grappling with the tension between autonomy and conformity, understanding how they might make a difference. But his voice must also resonate strongly with those artists, teachers and students craving to work in a supportive, creative learning environment, in which they can put their stamp on the world.

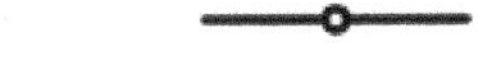

Testimony by Rick Holland, writer

I dealt with a peculiar extended trauma in early childhood that is not very fashionable, the dislocation of a young child at a boarding school. While I don't subscribe to revealing trauma as identity, I do recognise that this detail is formative, mainly in my case because it forced me to live in the margins in ways briefly described below.

I had some difficult experiences as a young person. My response was to decide very early to listen and only speak when I felt I had something valuable to say. I found escape in flow through sport, in music and in storytelling. I developed an early and very deep rooted affinity with 'Outsider' status and a resistance to unexplained authority. I continued to move regularly in adulthood and lived around the world. My storytelling developed into a career as a collaborating poet, working with some high-profile artists, and I lived several other careers alongside this main one.

My background defies easy identifiers. My mother's family are from the industrial working class of the North West, my father's family lived in service in Northamptonshire, but my Grandfather pushed into a middle-class world of clerical professional that led my father to Grammar school, and the Army, and a commission. I was given a scholarship and attended boarding schools from the age of 7 while my family was often abroad. The family moved around a lot.

I experienced institutions and types of people a long way removed from my family's social history. I also grew up with an ongoing dislocation from settled notions of 'home' and 'self', often experiencing lazy and unforgiving social judgement from all sides. It is probably no real surprise that I dislike and resist classification when I feel it isn't thought through, but also that I see very keenly the similarities in supposedly 'different' groups of people.

This life did allow me an unusual amount of unguided time as a very young person. It was hard for a number of reasons, though I was fundamentally safe, fed and watered, and very privileged in education terms. I think the space to think critically – 'from a distance' – has been the major formative element of this relatively unusual background. In simple terms, I didn't fit in. My family were from a working-class background. My experience had none of that sense of community, instead moving around with army postings and between boarding schools. All social groups I existed in judged other social groups that I also existed in. (...)

(...) I continue to write for many reasons, psychological, political, aesthetic, to make sense of the inner and outer world. I believe the motivation, deep down, is one born from that dislocation in childhood, and a wish to be noticed and appreciated, or even just heard in language from a pure source. The reasons for this outsider status are less important here than the acknowledgement of it as the principal driver in looking for creative expression, I think. Honouring this voice became the central driver, the 'purpose' of my life, as by living in contexts that didn't join up and by being 'different' in all the social groups I experienced, I was able to sit removed from and observe organisations and principles as diverse as the Army, public and private education settings, families, life in different countries, and imagine other societal disconnects from that 'outside' position. With the help of some mentors and some formative experiences, and a large dose of stubbornness and resilience, I have built a life that, in the main, honours my perspective. My purpose as a writer was to present experience as trigger for other people to spring into their own creative journey from, and my purpose as educator is very similar.

I fight to contribute to authentic culture. I try to listen to everything. This is tiring! I resist influencers that feel inauthentic. I try not to talk to them only in the terms of their authority but instead present my own findings and keep my skin as tough as possible. I try to remain open at all times to facing my own prejudices and default settings. I believe fundamentally that the skill sets I nurtured in myself have been of greater use than those prescribed to me in education, but also that I have been able to assimilate priceless lessons through meeting the particular challenge of any context and culture. Culture is live and complex. We need education to be too.

I came to teaching again from a 'successful' career as a creative, something that I self-managed, from writing to contracts and publishing. Contradictions and difficulties abound in a life as a truly 'creative' thinker within economic 'reality'. I was only partially successful in that career, or maybe as successful as it was possible to be, within those contradictions. The balance is incredibly hard to manage, between making and reflecting, improving as a practitioner and surviving in the world of money. Such pressures exist that make even putting work out into the world an achievement, and it is increasingly hard to keep the balance between the many different heads you need to use and the slow work of making something that is worthy of attention in the first place. I mention all this because the temptation for people coming back into a teaching environment (especially within an institution) is to use their own experience in becoming 'successful' as a blueprint. I see this happening so much. The good ones move away from this approach, or let their experience come through implicitly in genuine exchange that is based in the world of the 'student'. This approach can be hard to box up and categorise.

In reflection, from this difficult exercise of looking backwards, I would say maturity comes not in recognising your own outsider status, or in seeking out similarities to others, but in finding a place of openness that truly recognises complexity and flux. Discarding markers of status along the way. This is not 'tolerance', or even 'guidance', it is 'exchange' and once the business of exchange can happen untrammelled, and combine with practiced craft, purpose becomes lived, and motivation is possible in the face of the many challenges that will be placed in its way. Culture is made.

'Outsider' as label, a note

'Outsider' - categorically in art movement terms - represents those works made with no consciousness of market, or audience, or 'expertise'. I use it as identifier of thinking that happens outside of consensus culture, and of identification with ways of being that are marginalised.

The way I use it needs review too. Affinity with any label needs appraisal as life changes, it is not a fixed mark. In fact, writing reflectively like this allows it to be stripped again. But it remains one of my primary modes, the development of a kind of 'poetic painting' with few references to established schools, my own forays into making that don't hamstring themselves with too much self-conscious appraisal based on stylistics or aesthetics.

I hear something similar from so many of my students, and the reality is that 'research' - the business of building an artistic voice and appreciation of authentic artistic exchange in slow and long consumption of other works - is vital but cannot always be practiced convincingly or usefully directly alongside the 'making' of something, which really requires an abandon. Many students resist the 'reference' culture recognised in academia - I did too - as something that works against the making of their 'art'. It is one of the great challenges, balancing the input and the output, working on the full profile of yourself while avoiding a stultifying confusion of other inputs, especially if their message doesn't seem immediately relevant to your own contexts. Space is needed, this is messy work.

This is worthy of attention. There is no doubt that people benefit hugely from opening their frames of reference and developing an ability to position works critically within a bigger picture. My argument (leaning heavily on predecessors) is that this kind of critical work is enhanced infinitely by learning to trust and respect yourself as a maker, by continuing to make and present work even where its roots are not clear.

A longer piece of writing would go into the need for traditional academies to be challenged by new repertoire, new concepts of learning, new expressions, with a nurturing approach that offers time and space for the messy work. New ways are present in every classroom, however conscious of them the members are. It is the classroom itself that needs to adapt to find ways to make people aware of the contributions they are truly capable of.

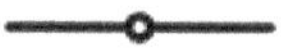

Rick writes in a compelling way that presents a challenge to arts institutions like conservatoires. But more fundamentally, his insights into his own childhood and subsequent development can only help to validate those many young artists seeking greater clarity and understanding of who they are. Such insight into roots, learning, becoming, knowing, creating, reflecting, opens doors for others in their own search for making sense of their life. It gives people permission to 'be' in a world bedevilled by endless 'doing'.

Michelle Tiwo, the Barbican Young Poet who wrote the poem *BLM (Black Lives Matter)* at the beginning of this chapter, provides two different perspectives on what it is to live a life that is not always in a welcoming world – a world in which identity has to be fought for.

Maybe I'll be the First
by Michelle Tiwo, Barbican Young Poet

*In the car shreds of 8am light pool, in the half-moons
under her eyes.
She tells me she's been searching all her life –
her spine now a heavy root, from years of reaching
and stretching and slipping to keep ends meeting.
She is a small tree in a big storm refusing to be displaced.
She doesn't always win. Then, anger has the habit of
burning hot coals in the pit of her stomach, splitting her
tongue into a lashing whip until black smoke blows
through her mouth.*

In her village, she tells me, she watched

many close to her fall. She tells me, when
she was young, there were murmurs of
dreamers hearing an oasis calling, whispering honey
as they slept and schemed. They let the sweetness drip
in deep waves. She says, she wants to experience just
once,
if it is as warm as those dreamers said.

For my mother, I am trying to learn what freedom looks
like
in this body of mine. What it tastes like in this mouth or
feels like running through the thick
of my hair and the small of my hands. I am trying
to grasp freedom with my teeth, the tips of my toes.
Trying to catch it on my eyelash,
for her.
She does not know freedom.
Has never known freedom
But I've seen it
Looking good, sauntering elsewhere.
I want it.
The choice to go
*Where I choose when **I am** ready.*

Ain't we worthy?

The End
by Michelle Tiwo, Barbican Young Poet

I have never fit in anywhere as easily as I fit behind these
books.
Behind this paper castle of novels and hardbacks. I
cannot save them today. The ceiling of this room a gaping
mouth of blank sky. The sun is as silent as my parents. As
silent as this ending. Cold water slicing at my toes as it
begins.

They are waiting for me to carry them to the other side,
where salvation waits on no one – like atheists waiting
on Christ.
The world is my tattered childhood bear falling to pieces.
It is coming. And I cannot save them. So I hide here.
My brother and sisters want me to play with them
before the world ends. Still I hide
in my paper fortress. They can't reach me.
I am the example. I should- could-
be leading them
to safety, above high water, somewhere
overlooking God's work and Her destruction...
but they
have made a sacrifice of me. So
I think I will stay
behind this tower
of books a little whi-

From all these reflections on identity one key element keeps recurring: the importance of 'connectedness', as a central pillar of how we see ourselves and the world. At one level it is impossible to understand the complexity of the world except through a broad prism that is enriched through its interconnections. On the other hand, for many younger people especially, the exponential rise of the internet and the burgeoning growth of social media make feelings of 'connectedness' little more than an illusion. This paradox is discussed robustly by Daisy Swift in her testimony, *The paradox of hyperconnectivity,and the power of music to connect us - for real.*

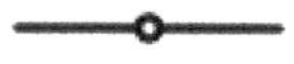

Testimony by Daisy Swift, Learning Director, Wigmore Hall, London

The paradox of hyperconnectivity

The internet has fostered literally billions of social connections. Our hyper-connected world enables us to always stay connected; we're always there — but does that make us less *here*? In the present moment with the people who are physically around us? Or is our idea of what *here* is changing? Are our physical and digital worlds coalescing, and if so what is facing us at the end of this collision course? I'm not going to pretend I have the answers to these huge and often overwhelming questions, but I can reflect on how some of these ideas have been made manifest in my life, and how I believe the arts, and in this case specifically music, can help.

I grew up during the birth of social media, so I have a kind of 'before and after' perspective. I remember that as a teenager, I used to spend hours on the phone to friends I'd seen all day at school. Today, in contrast, I find myself hiding behind busyness, doing seven things at once, connecting with seven people at once, and devouring 'fast content'; self-administering a sensory overload of information and entertainment. Phone in one hand, computer in front of the other.

Social media is an ostensibly connecting phenomenon, but the sad irony is that it can make our interactions ephemeral, superficial and filtered, and it has the power to disconnect and fragment our society. But it doesn't have to be that way. Surely a fundamental part of living a fulfilling human life is to connect with others? In some parts of the world, personhood is defined by the connections that an individual has with the people, places and things around them. That is, to be human is to be part of a network, connected. We are relational as well as individual; we're both. So, in a culture dominated by a multitude of online connections and seemingly fewer physical connections, how do we create a space in which we really connect, really listen, really respond?

That's where I believe music comes in. I mentioned I wanted to reflect on two personal experiences. The first is a music session with families living with dementia, in which we improvised together as a group. Connections sparked across the circle like impulses across synapses. Each person had a chance to conduct the musicians, and, when it was my turn, thirty-three years into my life, eleven years into my career, I experienced a feeling stronger than I had felt before: affirmation. I was being listened to, acknowledged, and responded to. More than that, my creative idea was being interpreted, developed; I could feel it growing like a tree! The sense of equality in that circle was astounding. Every individual – musician, person living with dementia, family member, myself – was treated as an equal in that space. I'd seen many times the incredible skill of musicians in this kind of context sensitively responding to the gestures, voices and music of people living with dementia, and it had always moved me to witness the power of these connections. But to be part of that experience – that community – made the experience vivid, technicolour.

Finding our voice

I've often reflected on whether I identify as a millennial (I am one, apparently), or an 'xennial' (yes, that's a thing now), and I've come to realise I don't, with either. Because we're all different. We should embrace our diversity rather than homogenising an entire generation of people and reducing ourselves to one word. I guess our desire to be part of a community, for kinship, kicks in; it gives our lives meaning and purpose and proves we're not just seven billion unconnected particles bouncing around the cosmos.

Millennials in particular seem to have a bad rap when it comes to this homogenisation. We are tagged with labels of laziness, entitlement, apathy … Eyes roll at the fact we can't buy houses because of our extravagant coffee and avocado habits … We are the generation of the selfie, often dismissed as vacuous and narcissistic. But aren't selfies just a way of telling the world we exist, an attempt to get our affirmation? In a photoshopped world the pressure is ever mounting to keep up with the illusion of perfection with which we are constantly bombarded. It terrifies me that self-worth is tied to likes, follows, favourites. How others perceive and receive us, rather than how we value and love ourselves. And it's not really *us* we're putting out there. We quite literally filter ourselves and our experiences to show the world a 'better' us; but it's an illusion. So how do we figure out who we are, what we believe in?

I can't really reflect on my own identity and perspective on music without writing about my experience of being a woman working in, and making, music. I believe that gender is a social construction we created to neatly categorise ourselves, and whilst it is a construction, it has a very real impact on us all. The categories we designed create an imbalance of power; they legitimise oppression and breed inequality. And in the case of gender, this power is the patriarchy. The arts – and its ability to empower, make confident, give voice – can be a powerful weapon against inequality. But women (let alone people who identify as trans- or non-binary) are massively underrepresented in the music industry, especially in positions of leadership. The overwhelming majority of songwriters, producers, conductors, composers, you name it – are male. So let's empower more women and girls to make and perform music; to be heard, listened to, validated.

This brings me to the second of my musical experiences, a band I play in. Every time we play I feel a sense of belonging, collaboration, fun, creativity, self-expression, empowerment. All those things, every time. And of course sometimes frustration and tiredness, but we feel it together. We make things and we are proud of them. We explore and express who we are, what we think and feel; we find our voices. And then we get to share those ideas with others, who support us, celebrate us. That's a very powerful feeling, and I want more people - more women - to have the opportunity to feel it.

So what next?

The Internet has of course connected us in so many ways, facilitated this globalised society. Social media has democratised conversation, democratised storytelling. And being able to access pretty much any kind of entertainment or information at the touch of a button is amazing. It enables us to participate more easily too: we can sign a petition in seconds from the comfort of our own homes. But when does 'clicktivism' become 'slacktivism'? Are we participating less, or rather with less depth, as a result of not having to make the effort? (...)

(...) Now at the risk of prising open another can of worms, this is a can I feel is important to open, an issue I need to confront: not all music-making engenders self-expression and connectedness. In contrast, some of the very structures that hold it up, that train our emerging musicians, can discourage, and even prohibit, exactly the kind of music-making I'm talking about. There is a hierarchy of so-called musical 'excellence', a perceived difference in status between genres and careers, an industry which says to our young musicians: to be the best you must focus on yourself, you must compete, and your success looks like a particular kind of career. For me this approach to music-making is deeply problematic; its *individual* rather than *relational* approach stands in stark opposition to the collaborative spirit that makes music so powerful, so important. There are passionate and committed individuals and institutions working hard to combat this culture, and I'm excited by the change, but it's a big one with a long journey ahead.

None of these issues are a quick fix; we're part of a cross-generational process, and the challenge is my generation has become accustomed to quick fixes. I think I need more moments of stopping, listening, responding — they are rare and should be valued, enabled. Music-making grounds us in the present, it forces us to really listen and respond to the person or people in front of us.

When we're up against feelings of alienation and uncertainty in a fractured world, making music together can help us to figure out who we are, and be empowered by that knowledge. Its power is in its ability to bring about self-expression, belonging and, ultimately, connectedness. I want to make my life about empowering people to find their unique, creative voices, and to use those voices to connect with the people around them.

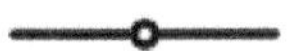

Daisy makes a very strong case for the importance of people finding genuine connection within a relational world that makes sense to them. For her shared music-making, the musical conversation with its collaborative spirit has become a central feature of her life. This is a far cry from the 'democratised' conversation provided by the social media that dominates the lives of so many young people.

It was encouraging to hear this view reiterated by two Drum Works Apprentices, Laurie Mann and Janki Makwana. Apart from being very committed members of Drum Works, they are both song-writers, exploring personal themes and stories. But it is Drum Works that gives them the social context where they relate to each other as a 'family'. Interviewed soon after the tragedy of the Grenfell Tower fire in London in 2017, when 72 people died, both Laurie and Janki vented their anger and disillusionment through their friends and social media. But they were also concerned by the illusion of being connected, acknowledging that many young people are content with the superficial feeling of connection. They prefer to see their friends more often in real life, not just through Instagram and Snapchat, where they can easily feel trapped. Just relying on social media can be damaging and both of them see it as toxic. They make a strong case for live music-making in a collaborative context, like Drum Works. This will be explored further in the next section.

THE ARTS: 'FAMILY' AND BELONGING

Barbican Young Poets

Icarus Lives
by Michelle Tiwo, Barbican Young Poet

I.
'06 ended with the newspapers that didn't care
publishing mugshot archives of young boys
who got merked over a postcode, a chick, their creps,
respect

Ego stabbed 'em or shot 'em, then left em fi dead, they
said.

Front page stories of almost-grown bodies spilling
their families' dreams down side street gutters or
into local park asphalts or
just somewhere for someone to find.
Like lost keys or
the Metro or
the one shoes left behind.

I wanted to kiss every photo printed
the way their mothers would kiss their foreheads
at the funeral procession.

Pictured these ghosts – some I hazily recalled from
parties in ends
I had no business in – laid in satin, ill-fitted death suits
hiding

exit wounds. Mothers wilting flowers over their ashen heads,
*crying: **My womb is a burial site after all my children are born.***

Papers said two mothers had buried other children, earlier that year.

II.
The year is 2018. Grief has caught you unexpectedly on the bus
home from work; you stand no chance.
You're barely aware of the audience in front of you
eavesdropping on your quiet weeping. Caught off guard,
you are a snuffled howl tucked into the back of the 168.

Maybe you will go home and smoke yourself numb, fall apart
in the arms of the duvet. Sleep with your teeth clenched.
Wake with a hollow rage in your chest.
Punch your pillows. Throw them. Repeat.

*Contemplate how bedrooms like bigger coffins we wake up and walk out of each day. Tell yourself, **"the show must go on, eat dammit"**. Smoke a spliff instead.*

Finally you leave the house, sun lightly caressing your forehead.
You cry, to your surprise, in the fruit and veg aisle of the Iceland
down the road – the weed has worn off and grief reminds you:
He was a lighthouse,
*   and they sliced through his flesh like the skin of the cooking tomato sitting in your*
*   palm.*
You imagine light spilling out of him. Imagine his enemies

momentarily blinded,
running in confusion –
was that the sun or God?

III.
What were you before you were born? A boy? A son?
A dream? A siren? A funeral hymn I learnt?

They screamed about your death the way Aunty in the
village will
when the news finally reaches her too – up and down the
street, arms a steeple
above her head, hands flailing red flags or
white ones, whichever signals the dead to return.
She'll howl until her voice becomes the hoarse shade of
sorrow,
until the wind catches on,
sends it round the village, then city, like harmattan dust.

For weeks I watched people choke on your name, sputter
stories after they could catch their breath, about how
you'd done so well to escape death the first time.

In sleep, heard your mother cry: will our wombs always
be a burial site after all our children are born?
Woke up to the Mayor of London declaring, he's not here
"to keep black boys safe" but
"to keep knives off the street".

I lay in bed.

All now, I want to hang in the sky a while too. Become the
Sun, maybe.
Everyday
Is a funeral prayer, it watches over. Everyday
is survival, it watches over.
And I no longer know if I want to burn here

In Babylon or
over it all.

IV.
There was a time I could say no-one I knew well had died.
This is not to suggest that no-one died.

Squares and Circles
by Kieron D. Rennie, Barbican Young Poet[11]

Around here
I hear the echoes of those,
saying I'll make things square.

My uncle once shared
that around here,
things were squared with fists
around here.

He told me about the various times
he did the Ali shuffle
in a scuffle.

How his
fist
did the tango in an opponent's face.

My father.

My father told me people were
popping and locking,
around here.

The Boom-box was rocking, around here.

---

[11] *Copyright © 6th January 2012, Kieron D. Rennie*

Looking around,
I see how things have changed.

Fists no longer tango
due volcanic egos that are prone to erupt.
Yeah, this is a serious issue
knives are now pushed in you exposing tissue.

Popping and locking is now forgotten.

It's all-out war
that many are locked in.

Borders are defined by postcode
entering another is a no go,
gang signs have become logos.

Around here,
Many vow it's an eye for an eye.

The same reason many die and many walk blind.

These two poems capture so poignantly two of the most disturbing and destructive aspects of urban society today – knife-crime and gang warfare. Many young people are angry, disillusioned and disengaged from a society that brings them nothing but negative feelings of inequality, injustice and alienation. Five years ago, under the auspices of the Barbican and Guildhall School, I published a Provocation Paper, *Being – In Tune*, which examined ways of addressing isolation and dislocation through engaging in the arts. (See Renshaw, 2013) Initially this was inspired by the powerful show, *Unleashed*, performed at the Barbican in November 2012, which was a creative response to the summer riots in London the previous year.

Boy Blue Entertainment and Drum Works

Many of the issues raised in that Paper are still germane today. In the discussions with Boy Blue Entertainment and Drum Works, key performers in *Unleashed*, time and again the benefits of working collaboratively in the arts were highlighted – from strengthening self-esteem and self-respect to developing a sense of belonging by breaking down feelings of alienation and isolation. Teamwork is critical to their ways of working and this is reinforced by a sense of family which binds people together. At its best this collective voice of 'family' helps to give young people a feeling of shared responsibility and it is hoped this prevents them from joining gangs and resorting to negative behaviour like knife-crime.

One of the things that stands out in the work of Boy Blue Entertainment, a Barbican Artistic Associate and Olivier Award-winning hip-hop dance company based in East London, is the raw energy, discipline, precision, dedication and confidence all the young people bring to their dancing. They are at the cutting edge of street culture, 'on the pulse' of what's happening and fearless in taking risks. Together they have created a learning community, a family with a strong work ethic sharing a similar perspective on life and holding similar values.

For Kenrick 'H2O' Sandy, Artistic Director and choreographer, and Michael 'Mikey J' Asante, Artistic Director and music producer, they see this belonging to 'family' as fundamental to the success of Boy Blue. It gives people a sense of connection and a feeling of identity. As Kenrick puts it:

> *For us, family is one the most important things. It's about being a part of something and the individual taking ownership of it. So if you're part of Boy Blue, understand it's not just about I'm in Boy Blue; it's about 'I am Boy Blue'. I am part of this crew and this crew is a part of me. From a social point of view they jam with each other, they*

go out with each other. You know, they look out for each other in the same way we look out for them. It's like we are kind of big brothers, uncles, dads to some of these kids because we have that kind of time. (Renshaw, 2013, p.11)

What is striking about Boy Blue is that they have created a holistic way of life in which there is unity between the artistic thrust of the company and its moral purpose – its concern for people and how they relate to each other and to the outside world. Its discipline, work ethic, drive, sense of shared responsibility and understanding of where young people are coming from can only help everyone to deal constructively with the pressures, challenges and expectations that might arise in daily life. It is impressive that Boy Blue has created a safe space, a nurturing environment, in which dancers can pursue their passion, but also one in which they can discover who they are in a supportive social group. There is no need for them to search for who they are in the context of a gang. Their sense of belonging, their self-knowledge is gained through their interaction within the group.

This was reiterated in a conversation with Chantelle, a committed 19-year old dancer at the time, who was convinced that her work with Boy Blue had helped to ground her, strengthen her self-esteem and given her a clear reference point with which to view her life.

[Boy Blue] has given me knowledge, skills and motivation, but it has also opened doors about understanding how others feel and interact within the group. Learning how to respond to these reciprocal relationships can only enhance the development of each person, and through the richness of my experience I have choreographed my own journey and that's a very strong element of who I am. (Renshaw, 2013, p.12)

Returning to my conversation with Laurie Mann, the Drum Works apprentice, it is clear that her commitment to Drum Works prevented her from spiralling out of control. She admitted that she hated school, she was difficult with teachers and she played truant – but she always turned up at the Drum Works sessions. In Year 9 her behavioural problems got much worse and Laurie was excluded from school. In Year 10 she was excluded for three months and sent to a Pupil Referral Unit. This very much upset her as she wasn't allowed to play in Drum Works while she was in the Unit. So Drum Works became her incentive for finishing her education and stopped her getting into more trouble. For Laurie one of the strongest aspects of Drum Works is its familial atmosphere. She felt alone without her friends, all of whom were in Drum Works. She contrasted this with the young people in the Pupil Referral Unit, all of whom were in gangs which reinforced their negative behaviour. In the end Laurie was 'saved' by her life in Drum Works and she is now going from strength to strength with her music.

Laurie's story well illustrates the mission of Drum Works which 'uses drumming as a tool to inspire creativity, build social cohesion and empower young people to direct their own futures'. This is reflected in its values[12]:

> *Personal: Drum Works is characterised by the strength of the personal connections forged at every level of the project; strong relationships exist between participants, artists, management, schools and other stakeholders.*
>
> *Responsive: we respond to participants' needs, make the most of opportunities and continually reflect on our work, allowing Drum Works to develop organically while maintaining its core ethos and identity.*
>
> *Open: we actively seek to collaborate and to share ideas.*
>
> *Participant-focused: all participants have a voice in the creative process and direction of the project; they have*

---

[12] https://drumworks.co.uk/who-we-are

ownership of it.
Proactive: *we are driven by our belief in the importance of positive action to create change.*
(Drum Works Strategic Plan, 2018-21, p.1)

These aspirations are reflected in the comments of students in the drumming group at Warren School, mentioned in Chapter 4. They were writing to the Headteacher to explain why Drum Works mattered to them. There were constant references to the importance of 'family', 'community', 'friendship', 'love', 'joy', 'happiness', 'enthusiasm', 'support' and 'inclusivity'. They felt that in their drumming sessions they were understood in a non-judgemental way, they gained in confidence, their memories were enhanced, new opportunities were opened up for them and any feelings of anger were calmed. One student sums it up this way:

> *Drum Works has made me see life differently. It has given me purpose in life that maybe I didn't feel I had in school. Sometimes in school I felt like teachers didn't listen to what I had to say, but in Drum Works everyone's voice gets heard. I've seen the quietest people be the loudest within one Drum Works lesson. This is because in Drum Works we never look at each other's backgrounds, but we see each other as family. Drum Works is not just about playing drums, it's about us developing as young adults and not giving up on our dreams. And that's why you shouldn't take away Drum Works, because you'd be taking away family.*

The voices of the Barbican Young Poets, Boy Blue Entertainment and Drum Works offer a strong testimony of what can be achieved by groups of young people pursuing their passion, unlocking their talent, pushing their boundaries and working together within a family of dedicated like-minded young artists. There's no doubt that each person has something significant to say. They wish to put their own stamp on the world, discover new possibilities and extend their horizons, both at a personal and collective level. At the heart of this is the 'family', with its strong sense of connectedness and belonging. Within this safe, yet dynamic framework, each person can flourish, balancing their creative energy with their response to the challenges of the outside world.

6

THE ARTS AND MENTAL HEALTH

This chapter explores some of the ways in which engaging in creative work can alleviate at least some of the pain of people suffering from depression, anxiety, anger, alienation, insecurity and loneliness – states of mind bedevilled by the strains and stresses of a dislocated society struggling to cope with austerity and poverty. At the time of writing, Professor Philip Alston (16 November, 2018), the UN's Special Rapporteur on extreme poverty and human rights, issued a Statement about his recent fact-finding mission on poverty in Great Britain. He stated that the country is suffering from "mean-spirited and often callous" austerity policies, noting how levels of child poverty are "not just a disgrace, but a social calamity and an economic disaster". (See Introduction)

Quoting figures from the Institute for Fiscal Studies and the Joseph Rowntree Foundation, Philip Alston stated that "about 14 million people, a fifth of the population, live in poverty, and 1.5 million are destitute, unable to afford basic essentials". He emphasised that the problems were "obvious to anyone who opens their eyes to see the immense growth in food banks and the queues waiting outside them, the people sleeping rough in the streets, the growth of homelessness, the sense of deep despair that leads even the government to appoint a minister for suicide prevention and civil society to report in depth on unheard-of levels of loneliness and isolation". He also commented that "he had met people who didn't have a safe place for their children to sleep, who had sold sex for money or shelter, young people who felt gangs were the only way out of destitution, and people with disabilities who were being told they needed to go back to work or lose support, against their doctors' orders".

These stark facts are the hallmark of a cruel and unjust society which can only be resolved through political intervention. Many local councils supported by charities are desperately trying to find creative solutions in order to help vulnerable people survive, but despite these initiatives increasing numbers are suffering from mental health problems, depression and feelings of fear and loneliness.

Engaging in the arts, working together with others on creative activities, are not going to solve these major social issues, but there is mounting evidence that they can provide moments of respite and offer positive ways of finding personal fulfilment that can help build up self-respect, resilience and a sense of connection.

This was discussed at the beginning of Chapter 5 when reference was made to the research findings of the Durham Commission on Creativity and Education (2019) and the Youth Music Report (2019) *The Sound of the Next Generation.* The Durham Commission highlights the critical issue of child and adolescent mental health, and it emphasises the positive outcomes that can be achieved by engaging in creative activities. It highlights two important statements:

The UK Youth Parliament has called for an improvement on mental health services led by young people along with the placement of such services in schools. They also advocate a shift in education practice to deliver on compulsory health education, promoting inclusion of the voice of young people and supported by creative thinking and creative expression. (ibid., p.41)

The All-Party Parliamentary Group for Arts, Health and Wellbeing, informed by the 2017 Creative Health report, met in February 2019 specifically to discuss the arts and child/adolescent mental health, including within and outside of schools. There was a strong consensus about the contribution of creative activity and self-expression to building confidence and resilience, as well as the use of creative interventions and activities in addressing specific challenges such as depression and anxiety. (ibid., p.41)

Again, the Durham Commission demonstrates that young people feel that engaging in the arts especially promotes a sense of personal wellbeing, alleviating feelings of stress and anxiety.

Although the Commission concludes that creativity and creative thinking can make an important contribution to improving wellbeing, including mental health, it recognises that these benefits are most strongly associated with creativity involving arts and cultural activities, which are less available in school to the young people who might benefit the most from them. Subjects such as art and design, dance, drama and music should be a significant part of the in-classroom curriculum for all children and young people. We should be particularly concerned when it comes to the lessening of opportunities for young people facing disadvantage. (ibid., p.42)

The Youth Music Report (2019) also embraces that music is a powerful contributor to wellbeing and mental health.

> *Exam pressures, a volatile external environment and technological and social change, in particular social media, are all linked to young people's wellbeing. Listening to music makes most people feel happy, and the effects of making music are even more powerful than listening to it. Young people are deploying music to articulate and communicate their thoughts and feelings. Music helps to form friendships which results in an increased sense of belonging. Those who regularly make music feel more in control of their future. Young people are using music as a tool to support their wellbeing. (ibid., p.4)*

Three further statements from the Youth Music Report (2019) illustrate the important link between engaging in music and a young person's wellbeing:

> *There is significant research demonstrating the power of music in improving mood and aiding in the treatment of health issues. Music-making has been shown to diminish anxiety, stress and self-harm; and to increase communication and coping strategies for young people in child and adolescent health settings. (ibid., p.16)*

There is growing evidence that engaging in music can help to combat loneliness.

> *Young people are more likely than any other generation to be lonely, with 10% of people aged 16 to 24 identifying as 'always or often' lonely, three times higher than people aged 65 and over. Indeed, a high percentage of young people in our research reported that they felt lonely. Those who made music in the last week, however, were less likely to say they 'often feel lonely'. (ibid., p.16)*

Most importantly the Report made explicit the significance of the link between participating in music and strengthening a feeling of social cohesion, and a sense of connectedness and of belonging.

> *Regular participation in group musical activities can strengthen social cohesion by increasing empathy and cooperative behaviour. Making music in groups has wider social value – besides the development of individual friendships – by providing 'opportunities to communicate and connect with other people' and a sense of belonging.* (ibid., p.18)

The remainder of this chapter provides examples of the power of music and the arts in the lives of a number of courageous young people determined to address their mental health difficulties through unlocking their own creative energy. It remains for artists to recognise the role they could play in an area that remains uncharted for many. This presents a major challenge for many artists and arts organisations.

WORLD OF SELF-CARE

Many theatre companies take their responsibility in the area of mental health seriously as drama is a very positive way of enabling young people to work together creatively and strengthen their self-esteem. One such example is the Chickenshed Theatre Company in London which creates the kind of supportive environment in which young people can feel accepted and express themselves without being judged. For Georgia Dodsworth, a former student on the Performance & Creative Enterprise programme at the Guildhall School of Music & Drama, Chickenshed was the safe space she needed to stabilise and grow in strength. Between the ages of 12 and 17 Georgia suffered from anxiety, depression and later from ME, which led her to have suicidal and self-harming thoughts. For several years there were regular visits to the doctor, hospital and the NHS's

Child and Adolescent Mental Health Services (CAMHS), and when she was 17 she received a diagnosis of borderline personality disorder. Whilst Georgia's commitment to theatre was her lifeline, she also realised that she had to learn to become responsible for her own mental health. So much so that she gave birth to a movement called World of Self-Care. In an article she wrote for *Happiful* (a magazine devoted to mental health) Georgia makes a strong statement about the importance of self-care:

> *This is why self-care is so important to me and has become a massive part of my everyday routine. It's about taking the time out to make small actions that benefit your mind, body and soul. Self-care is unique to everybody, as it's about tuning in to what you need – not what society is telling you. Practising self-care is a challenge, but over time it does become a habit.*
>
> *Witnessing the effects of self-care first-hand has inspired me to start a movement: World of Self-Care – a platform exploring self-care, self-love and mental wellbeing through art-based workshops and discussions. The response has been overwhelming, and I hope one day I can go into schools and educate teachers and students on mental health and the importance of self-care. (Happiful, April 2018, pp.38-39)*

THE PLACE OF CREATIVITY IN MENTAL HEALTH

Lauren Saunders, the enterprising visual artist working in Hull, whose views struck a chord in Chapter 5, explored the place of creativity and making art in the area of mental health for her BA Dissertation at Hull School of Art and Design. Drawing on her dissertation her testimony makes explicit the ways in which creative engagement can make a qualitative difference to the life of a young person.

———o———

Testimony by Lauren Saunders, visual artist

Art really helps me manage my moods and emotions and it has done for a very long time; without sounding dramatic, I would probably be dead if I didn't have Art. Making is a cathartic process, full of meaning and depending on the situation, full of distraction and/or full of reflection. For my BA Dissertation, I wrote about the relationships between the visual arts and meaningful mental health recovery.

Inspired by my experiences of mental health and facilitating/running art groups within the NHS, I researched into what makes Art a therapeutic recovery-orientated activity. Within my dissertation, multiple approaches were applied to examine the complex relationship between art and mental health. I focused on the role of art activity in mental health recovery, how it aligns with the 'Recovery Approach' and existing and potential applications within clinical and personal contexts. I drew upon research across disciplines as well as conducting first-hand research and reviewing first person perspectives. After investigating the development of 'absolute' clinical understanding and popular opinion regarding mental health, I examined artist responses to ask if artwork can help to change and shape social attitudes, and investigated the impact of therapeutic art upon Western clinical psychiatry.

I used philosophical, psychological and sociological theories about creativity to establish how art could be utilised within mental health recovery and examined clinical research into the efficacy of therapeutic art. I analysed first-hand research sourced through the production of a special exhibition, statements from services users and staff, observational case studies with psychiatric in-patients and an artist interview, in order to compare this new qualitative data to existing research. I also presented my own critical conclusions and proposed strategies for implementing creativity within organised and personal care.

There were a few observations I found through research that I feel illustrate and support how creative engagement can make a qualitative difference in a young person's life:

- Informal drop-in and inclusive arts activity provision could build trust between communities and services.
- Artists can, have, and will continue to challenge the stigma surrounding mental health by sharing and expressing their experiences through art-making, consciously or otherwise.
- Independent engagement with arts provision promotes control within a meaningful, satisfying life.
- Art is a powerful tool in promoting a meaningful life to those experiencing mental difficulties; it provides the forum for achievable goal-setting and symptom management and control, opportunities for increased self-esteem, confidence and self-awareness.
- The appreciation and identification of successful artists with lived experience can inspire hope and meaning.
- Art-making creates a visual vocabulary in which people can share their experiences to guide others and to educate.
- Art may not be a 'cure' for mental health, but it can make life significantly more manageable and can be an effective way to communicate internal realities and experiences to oneself and to the world.

People find a voice through the Arts. They find their own voice, find similar voices and use that voice to communicate their realities and/or speak out against the 'man'. In my recent Fine Art practice, my work has used a philosophical and mindful approach to question how I experience the world. This has been an invaluable experience for me. I feel that months of exploring the subject has allowed my voice and my confidence as an artist to develop. Moving forward, I intend to use my art, my voice, to speak out against the injustices I see in the world both practically, through funded projects and work, and visually through the production of work itself.

———o———

This could not be a clearer exposition about the positive role of art-making, of creative engagement, in the lives of people with mental health challenges. Soon after graduating Lauren Saunders (2019) along with Jill Howitt launched a new journal, *The Critical Fish*[13], with the support of Arts Council England and Hull City Council, amongst others. In their Mission Statement the Commissioners state that "Fish is a journal promoting research-led writing about arts and visual culture centred on Hull and the region. The publication will be a forum for debate; connecting organisations, artists and audiences. We will feature critical but accessible writing and support creativity and culture in the city and surrounding area". This is a strong example of 'youth voice' determined to make a difference in the world through the arts – practical, reflective, dynamic, local but drawing on global perspectives.

THE IRENE TAYLOR TRUST

One organisation I've been closely connected to for many years is The Irene Taylor Trust, referred to briefly in Chapter 4. Its three key programmes – Making Tracks (including Young Producers), Music in Prisons and Sounding Out[14]:

> *… support young people at risk, people of all ages in prisons, and ex-prisoners rebuilding their lives on release. Creating original music collaboratively can make a powerful impact on people's lives, bringing them new confidence, important transferable skills (such as communication, team-working, problem-solving and perseverance) and raised aspirations for the future. We work with some of the most disadvantaged and marginalised individuals in our society, having faced a range of issues, such as abuse, violence, substance misuse, mental health problems, exclusion from school*

---

[13] www.thecriticalfish.co.uk
[14] www.irenetaylortrust.com

and homelessness.
The Irene Taylor Trust, Annual Report, 2016-17, p.3

In conversation with two young people, Abdul (18) and Helen (19), on the Making Tracks programme, it was clear that writing and music was a positive force for good in their lives.

Abdul, participant Making Tracks and Young Producers

In his mid-teens Abdul had to take on more responsibilities at home because changes were taking place within the family. He felt his life lacked structure and that he couldn't process what was going on. This led to him suffering from stress and depression at school, shifting from being outgoing to a more introspective person. As things got worse and he could no longer focus on studying for his GCSE examinations, his doctor referred him to the Childhood Adolescent Mental Health Service (CAMHS) who sectioned him in hospital several times during his 17th year. Abdul acknowledges how much he benefitted from the opportunity to talk through his difficulties with skilled mental health professionals and then he found further support from The Prince's Trust, whose activities enabled him to focus more on his own personal development. In discussion Abdul felt that it has been important to share his thoughts with others. This was not about gaining attention but by speaking out this might help other people as well. He had come to the conclusion that "in order to help yourself, help others" and that "you have to focus on yourself before you focus on others and give back".

Through The Prince's Trust, Abdul became involved with The Irene Taylor Trust who gave him the opportunity to further develop his writing and music. Whilst in hospital his writing gradually shifted from a therapeutic response to depression to a more positive engagement with his creativity through poetry, lyrics, music and rap. Making Tracks and the Young Producers gave Abdul the opportunity to bring his material to life with a band. Bouncing off this positive experience he now aspires to make more music for himself and then to share this with others. Eventually he wants to have his own studio, working with young people and developing his own musical community.

Conversation with Helen, participant Making Tracks and Young Producers

My conversation with Helen, in conjunction with Lauren Reid (at the time Personal Development Coordinator of The Irene Taylor Trust), was especially illuminating and it offers a strong justification for encouraging young people with mental health issues to engage in some kind of creative, artistic activities. When asked how she feels about her life at the moment, Helen responded:

Helen *I feel I have now come to the point of 'acceptance' – accepting things that have happened in the past and how they have shaped me to be the person I am today. It has taken me 19 years to get there but I have reached a point where people might call it radical acceptance or a coming to terms, but the nature of my personality, my illness, the world around me is unstable and changing constantly. For years I tried to fight against it and tried to make my own way out of it, but sometimes in some situations you just have to go with it, accepting that you can't always juggle everything as you want to, and things aren't always going the way you want them to – and that's okay.*

PR *What has brought you to this acceptance?*

Helen *I never felt in control of my life. My mother died of cancer when I was four. I was not brought up by my father, which was very tricky. I had traumatic experiences in my childhood and as I matured in age and reached my early teens, I started to fight back for the control I thought I deserved.*

Unfortunately, I couldn't influence everybody and everything around me, or even myself, in the way my brain became programmed and I dealt with difficulties in my life. My brain was programmed just to self-destruct. My way of coping with things was to be angry, not with others, but with myself. I just had a mental block at being able to accept things, to accept that at times horrible things do happen. I think that what made it harder for me was that on the outside it appeared that I came from a middle class family, and I had a lot of people around me, but when you dug a little bit deeper it became very tricky. Appearances were kept up by certain people in my life, but these appearances hindered my chances of getting help when I needed it.

About two years ago I came to terms with a lot of repressed memories that suddenly resurfaced and I got into a really bad state. First I went through a phase of anger and I began to grieve for the first time in my life – not only for my Mum and other people who had passed away, but also for a childhood I'd never really had and for the opportunities I missed along the way. I suddenly became so angry to the point I couldn't feel any other emotions. In therapy I didn't even have the words to express it. I was like this for a while and landed up in some really awful situations again. Then I realised there was no point in holding on to this anger as it was eating me alive. I couldn't have continued if I'd continued to feel like that, so I realised there was not much I could do except roll with it, to ride out the waves.

I started therapy when I was 10. In therapy there is a lot of talk about 'riding out the waves', 'riding out the pain', but it never really made sense until I suddenly got to the point when I realised that there was nothing I could do. I had totally given up my sanity and all I could do now was 'to ride it out'. By beginning to realise this, I gradually began to accept my past and my present. And if I ride out this wave I might even have a future. I realised that I had to go with this – 'to sink or swim'. 'Water' became a metaphor. By the age of 18 I'd spent a year of my life in psychiatric hospitals. The number of near-death experiences I'd had at this time was enormous....

PR   *What role did The Prince's Trust and The Irene Taylor Trust play in your 'recovery'?*

Helen   *I think what I've noticed, not just with myself, but also with other people through The Irene Taylor Trust and The Prince's Trust, is that most people who go through difficult situations at a young age know that something needs to change. They need to know that other options are available, and I think bodies like The Irene Taylor Trust and The Prince's Trust are trying to reach out into areas where other systems aren't. But there are still a lot of people who are confused and are unreachable at the moment.*

I think once given a choice a lot of people will make the right or best choice, although this depends on the person and the circumstances. But a lot of people are not given the choice. I feel if you don't know, you can't make an informed decision in relation to the social work system or the mental health system. As soon as you are 18 you are seen as accountable for your whole life. Nothing you do is ever to do with others – it's always 'you'. A lot of people have been told that they've made informed choices, but they haven't. You are talking about families who have a history of things – how are you to live any better when you've lived with people telling you that this is the way it is?

I think a lot needs to be done if people can't be reversed. What matters is that you come to the point where you make a life-changing decision and you then have that on your record or you've got people who won't trust you anymore. The severity, of course, varies. There comes a point where it becomes permanent and there are things I would try to make up for the rest of my life, but they are still there and will always be there. It's so important that people are becoming more involved and involved at a younger age.

There is always the 'what if'? What if, when I first started experiencing flashes and things – what if I had received bereavement therapy at the beginning? But now I'm at the point where I've got therapy, I've got this and I've got that, and now I have to deal with what's going on. But the harder everyone works to understand things and to make other people understand, there won't be people like me still asking 'what if'?

PR   *Do you feel that this fairly recent point of 'acceptance' is one major step in not relying on external agencies? You are now taking on full responsibility, not blame, for yourself, for your own development, personal life and your future professional life. The ball is now in your court and you feel a sense of agency.*

Helen   *Yes! I love that word – 'agency' – it's my favourite word.*

PR   *You've got it!*

Helen   *Yes, for the first time in my life….*

PR   *How did The Prince's Trust and Making Tracks come your way?*

Helen   *It was a bit weird actually because I had just finished my residential with The Prince's Trust. When you first start at Fairbridge with The Trust (The Prince's Trust Fairbridge Programme), you go camping for about two days in the middle of nowhere. When we returned we were told of another project that had just turned up – Making Tracks. Many of the group liked rapping etc., but I thought 'what?'!*

PR   *How old were you at the time?*

Helen   *16 – when I was young, Year 2 at school, I had passed Grade 2 Piano. I'd been good at music in terms of piano at a young age, but after things changed I had to stop. I didn't touch the piano after that. A couple of years before I was 16 I started to write poetry. I look back at the poetry I wrote then and say 'Gosh, I can't believe I wrote that stuff. It's so cringey, so dark'.*

I'm just surprised people read it and didn't say 'how deeply disturbed is this girl!' It was awful, some of it. It was my innermost thoughts. It was so dark and raw – but not raw in an artistic way. I wanted someone to notice how awful things were. Of course, no one did! Then someone in The Prince's Trust said 'why don't you give Making Tracks a go?' I knew a couple of people who were doing it and I thought, 'why not'. So I decided to give it a go.

On the Monday morning we sat in a circle in St. Mark's Church with the project team – Nick, Rex, Charles and Gary – plus the participants. I ended up writing some poetry/lyrics which we performed at the end of the project. I also ended up singing which I hadn't really done before. I remember on the evening of the gig having a complete freak out about it. Hermione, (the Personal Development Coordinator at the time), said – 'just give it a go; no one is here to judge you'.

For the first time in my life I realised it was true. People were coming to the gig because they wanted to. Most of the things in my life I had been guilt-tripped into doing, and suddenly here I was being able to make my own decisions without any influence of guilt or feeling I owe people things. This was such a freeing experience.

So I then came back as a mentor on Making Tracks projects. But then things got worse again and I ended up going into my year-long admission. During my admission I turned 18 and I was placed in an open psychiatric ward. Whilst there, I experienced the feeling of 'no-fixed abode'. I much prefer that term because there is still a stigma around the term 'homelessness' – meaning if you're homeless, you're on the streets. And that's so not the case. There's an almost secret world of hostels, bed and breakfasts. It's ugly, it's not something that people want to talk about and know about....

.... I was suddenly thrown into this world where I was living with anyone between the ages of 18 and 65 with mental health

difficulties. This was a world I hadn't been exposed to before. Adolescent mental health is very closed off between the ages of 12 and 17. In an adolescent ward both patients and staff hope that you'll recover from your illness. And then when you're placed in the adult system your hope seems to go immediately. Suddenly everything is your fault. If you do something it's because you're irresponsible and stupid. It's not because you're ill or struggling. And so I was living in a house with these people in supported 24-hour accommodation and it was pretty like being in a hospital. I was not getting better. I was having the police call on me whenever I left. I was really unwell and so I started going in and out of adult wards. Actually when I started the Young Producer project with The Irene Taylor Trust in 2017 I was admitted to hospital.

Lauren *You came and did the performance as well from hospital. You must have been having such a hard time. I remember you calling me saying sorry this has happened. Of course you had nothing to apologise for. We just wanted you to be okay and to get the support you needed.*

PR   *In what way did this Making Tracks experience affect your life?*

Helen   *Before Making Tracks I hadn't ever considered engaging in making music. I listened to music, I played the piano, I wrote poetry, but I had never ever thought about making music. And suddenly I was able to express things and I feel like it's more socially acceptable. If I was to sit here and say certain things, or they were to appear in a piece of rap or popular rap music where they often speak about drugs and all of that, people will sing along even if they don't know what they're talking about or they don't understand it – it's cool or it's good music. But if someone were to sit down and talk about one of these things in a coffee shop or from person to person, it would suddenly be 'what are you doing?' – 'how dare you!'*

So suddenly I had a way of being able to express myself without worrying about people stopping and going 'what's your problem?' Suddenly I was able to explain things and I think it was the beginning of being able to express myself about things that had happened in the past.

One of the first songs I ever wrote, 'Origami Hearts', brought up a lot of stuff that I hadn't brought up before – 'Long tops are here again' or 'The Pain'. In the Summer having to walk around in jumpers or long-sleeved tops – what! – but with no one bothering to explain or ask if this was okay. 'The Pain' talks about someone who abused me. The whole song was about complicated, difficult relationships within myself, and between me and other people. What I loved was this kind of idea of the fragility of paper and the chorus 'Origami Hearts Unfold'. It opened up everything that had been so perfectly folded away – stories that were never told.

PR   *Did you find the whole process unlocked your voice, gave you permission to enter your previous world? Was it a very therapeutic experience?*

Helen *When people say 'music is my therapy', it really was for me. Suddenly, through music I connected with so many people. A lot of my life I have been slipping through gaps to avoid social services or to avoid hospitalisation. I tried! I was focusing all my energy on avoiding all these things and I didn't feel I fitted in or connected to anyone particularly. I didn't build healthy strong relationships. I was so focused on what I was doing I ended up forming really unhealthy toxic relationships.*

And then through music I was suddenly thrown into a bunch of people who otherwise I would never have really met. But I suddenly found a mutual connection that goes deeper than 'I'm ill – you're ill – let's be ill together. You've been through hard times, so have I'; and we both write about it and enjoy the creative aspects of music. I suddenly started forming real relationships. I was thinking, 'how can it be so easy?' But it was.

Music became my safe space. No matter where I was or what was going on around me, I knew if I walked into something similar, I'd feel safe. No matter who was in the room with me, I'd still feel safe.

PR   *Do you think that feeling helped you to reach this point of acceptance which you're now so clear about? – acceptance of who you are, acceptance of the past, acceptance of the world around you, acceptance of people, beginning to trust yourself before trusting other people – because you have to have that self-love in a way in order to trust others?*

Helen *I think all of them. Through music I've been able to express things, not only to others but also to myself. Things like the exercises; having to write down things on paper, somehow it's more permanent. It's 'there' now; it's out in the world, it's not in my head anymore. It's externalised. So I've learnt as if I've been reading things, almost as an outsider. Sometimes I was in such a state that I would disassociate myself and write lots of stuff and come back to the real world. Then I say, 'Oh my God, what is this?' It's a really weird kind of experience to have.*

PR   *Who do you share this with?*

Helen *Not many people. I think if there's a project I'll write something. I might kind of use it.*

PR   *But there's ongoing writing now?*

Helen *Ongoing, but I don't tend to share it. I think I get this burst of inspiration through a difficult period – like in my long admission when I wrote six songs – six complete songs!*

PR   *Have you considered forming your own group so that you could share your creative work together?*

Helen *I think for me a lot of it is kind of insular. I'm still coming* *to terms and trying to accept. Sometimes I need that push that we have to produce five songs by whenever and then push myself to do it and share these things. And when I do, I feel so much better. I still find at times that I need that push. Music really has become a constant in my life. At first I didn't realise it, but I viewed the people in The Irene Taylor Trust as a constant and they've also introduced me to music which will be with me all the way through my life.*

It's one of those things that's always there, almost physically – on my phone, recordings and things I've been working on. I have a notepad in my bag. Also I may be sitting somewhere and I think 'oh, that would sound really good'. So I then write it down somewhere. It's become a walking, talking toolbox for me – something that I can get out when feeling stressed or something. From a young age I was always told by people not to talk up, not to speak out, that I didn't have anything important to say – so I didn't really have a voice. Or it's like I hadn't discovered my voice.

PR   *But you have a voice now and it would be helpful to share this with others rather than just keeping it to yourself.*

Lauren *It sounds as if this has been a journey in terms of hearing that voice – and may be the journey is more about getting it out. I feel it's coming out more and more; it's going to become more powerful.*

Helen   *When I write a song I write it all out, and then I refine it, I work on it, I think of different words that may sound more useful. The voice I have learnt, I have. When I first started it was more like poetry – it was so jumbled, painful, even reading it was painful. I've now learnt how to tailor it slightly, to make it more therapeutic, and to make it easier for others to understand.*

PR   *You don't find your artistic language overnight! It's a long, long journey and you'll keep refining it – the subtle nuances of language.*

Helen   *Yes, and I think people forget that.*

Soon after this extraordinary lucid and honest conversation Helen wrote a poem that so well illustrates her shift from 'falling' to 'flying' – a positive moment on her journey to acceptance.

Falling
by Helen

It's cold, but I've been colder
Here we go, further down the line
Might be choking on my fingers
I'll be fine
Take away my freedom
Weaponise me, but you'll see
You can take it all away
The fall is mine

Because I'm falling
Past the point of no return
Falling back to earth
Falling far from you
And I'm mourning
Like a child, just can't stop crying
See your face, and I'm transported
Back to you

These nightmares are getting old
A younger me, same old dream
This time, I'll nod my head
You'll be fine
Dust myself off, start again
Rising from the ashes
Of the bridges we have burnt
The fall is mine

Because I'm falling
Falling back to earth
Falling far from you
Now I'm flying
Eyes closed, arms wide open
Past the point of no return
A soaring heart that can't be broken
Not by you

Perhaps 'rising from the ashes' could be seen as a metaphor for young people with mental health difficulties searching for fulfilment through their engagement with the creative process. Helen expresses this so well, but she also recognises the crucial part played by the musicians she worked with from The Irene Taylor Trust. The wide-ranging breadth of their musicianship, the richness of their creative palette, their artistic integrity, their flexibility, sensitivity and sheer sense of grounded humanity lie at the core of what they bring to each project. The musicians working in such challenging contexts would never claim to be acting as 'therapists', although their work might be very therapeutic for all participants. Nevertheless, any creative process has the potential to unlock memories and feelings that might have been buried for some time, and that might have consequences for the young participants who might benefit from further support. In the case of The Irene Taylor Trust this extra-musical support is provided by the Personal Development Coordinator. At the time of writing this position was held by Lauren Reid, who discusses her supportive role in her testimony.

Testimony by Lauren Reid, Former Personal Development Coordinator, The Irene Taylor Trust

In my role at The Irene Taylor Trust, I have had the privilege of witnessing countless moments where someone's life has changed for the better. This has primarily been through engaging in our music projects. Whether it is music or the arts in broader terms, I really believe in it as a medium to transform an individual's purpose and path. Personally, I feel that there are specific elements about the process of engaging with music, especially as a group activity, which enable this to happen at a fast speed. Music unites us and as one participant described to me, "music is a language that helps individuals to communicate with one another, no matter where they're from or what life experiences they've had".

The way most of our music projects work includes being with a group for two weeks, working with professional musicians, exploring playing different instruments, writing original music, recording, performing, exploring music production, DJing and spoken word. This project is called Making Tracks. My role during these projects is to create a relationship with individuals, supporting them through the project and listening to their passions and interests. I then work to support them to pursue their interests on a long- term basis following the project. During the times when they are engaging with the musicians and developing their skills, I observe their development. Someone will bring an idea in and then suddenly the idea will spring to life, evolving into a chord progression or a lyric and then eventually a whole song. These organic moments you can't capture in numbers or figures. It is the vital process that is slowly developing someone's skills, talent, creativity and aspirations and supports them to form relationships and bonds with others and work as a team.

Usually, a young person will come with a lyric in mind as a starting point. One of the musicians will hear it/ see it and support them to arrange the words in musical form. In many instances the lyrics and words we hear from the young people are dynamic, passionate, wise and often traumatic. They use writing as a form of expression to digest their own struggles and complexities in their lives. One of the key things I've witnessed through their engagement in music is the space to speak about things that otherwise one would never know. Whilst developing their communication through the lyrics they write in the songs, you hear untold stories that have never been told before, a snapshot into their lives and what they are dealing with, and watch them process things that they haven't tapped into previously.

I am also able to see great untapped talent flourish. I remember one participant who took part in a Making Tracks project whom we met whilst running it in a Youth Offending Service. I knew nothing about the young person's life previously other than what they told me in passing. When they started to rap I was blown away. This quiet, shy individual that struggled to say two words to me had something to say!! All we had to do was put a microphone in front of them and it came out. Their talent certainly took the stage but also their voice was so strong, passionate and mature beyond their years. It scares me to think, what if that individual didn't have that space to express themselves!

I remember when we started working with another young person they were in the process of resitting exams due to previous mental health issues. They used poetry as a form of therapy and had reams and reams of writing. We supported them to bring their words to life and make songs out of them. They had never performed before or made music. I then worked with them to engage in a local studio post project and there they were able to work with producers and continue making music. Even though their family did not support their career path, in their heart they had found their true calling and aspired to make music one day. As time passed their confidence grew alongside their skill and talent. It showed that in that moment during the project, through finding their passion for music, they had found an end goal, a purpose and fulfilment.

When Helen first came into contact with The Irene Taylor Trust, it was before I was in the role I am now. She took part in a Making

Tracks project and then came back as a peer mentor on other projects between the ages of 16-17. She was struggling with her mental health and understanding her context, her environment and traumas she had suffered. When reflecting on this intervention, she says music wasn't something she had considered previously but found it was a space to express herself in a way she hadn't before. Being part of a Making Tracks project created a safe environment for her to feel socially accepted in a way she hadn't felt before, with people she had never met, doing something she had never done before. Helen's battle with her mental health continued for many years following this intervention and she herself discusses her own path with her mental illness as something she will always be aware of living with.

When I came into the role as Personal Development Coordinator, she was in hospital at the time. It was a difficult position to work from as I was developing a relationship with her off the back foot of our previous intervention, but the foundations that had been laid were very strong and quite clearly of benefit to her process. I was aware that for her it was about creating an environment of safety, for her to know that I am there to support her with what she needs, when she needs it and that I am not there to judge her process. The door is always open. So, we kept inviting her to be part of various little musical interventions, making her aware to go at her own pace but also holding her hand and giving her little pushes when necessary. Supporting her to continue expressing herself, shining in her own way and creating a network of support she can fall back on. I think allowing her the space to lead and guide us has been important for her and the relationships we have formed. It's important to understand that this work is not a 'quick fix' and sometimes it can take years. The wrap around support around the project is as valuable as the music itself. It may be the start of unlocking something and understanding where the individual needs to go next, keeping flexible and in-tune with this wherever you are supporting them to head, it is at their pace and rhythm.

Whilst working on one of our Making Tracks projects I remember an incident where a police officer came into the project who had arrested a participant previously. Even before she stepped into the space, she said that she and the participant had 'issues'. When the police officer came into the room, the participant was playing drums and the police officer was completely shocked and said, 'he looks like a child'. The participant was 16 at the time; I had to remind the police officer that he was a child. This connection was not only important for their relationship, but also for the perception and judgement of the participant. The police officer had seen the participant in a different context and had become desensitised to the fact that they were a child. Now, they were seeing the participant playing music, they could see them in a more playful situation and relate a little more easily to their vulnerabilities. They remembered that they were just a child. Some of the situations that the participants are processing outside of the space are very complex and chaotic. Through the process of music they can come into the space, focus and play as children again.

When reflecting on these successes, the environment that is created is of key importance. I think that both my role and that of the project team (musicians leading the sessions) are vital in understanding the dynamics of the space and participants we are working with. I think music is a powerful tool to unlock many things in a person and create relationships that otherwise might not have flourished. Music is used as a tool to communicate without words, sharing an experience, encouraging and supporting the individual to tap into an unknown part of themselves, which can be extremely transformative. It is important to respect and listen to their voice without judgement and make sure the space is safe to express themselves during an experience which can leave them feeling quite vulnerable. When the environment is safe it can support individuals to step into the unknown, building a sense of community, taking part in something unknown, encouraging them to take a leap and to support them to do so and this in turn supports a growth in confidence and belonging.

Personally, in my own educational development, I've felt first-hand how the arts can support a young person to achieve and thrive. I found all subjects other than dance, drama and music, quite difficult at school and was left feeling disheartened and unconfident in my abilities. But the arts were something where I felt accomplished; I felt creative and able to express myself. Every young person is different, and I think our educational system sometimes fails individuals by disallowing the space or encouragement to explore, learn and develop their individual potential talents or learning styles. I have said to myself countless times that if it wasn't for the arts, for my access to creative subjects, school would have been a miserable place for me and I don't think I would have gone as far as I did academically. It is so important for people to access the arts especially if they are disengaging from life, school and ultimately themselves. To find their 'north star' is the biggest anchor that I have seen to shield against what life throws at them.

With that in mind, this work is very personal for me and I am tremendously grateful for being able to support young people through those transitions.

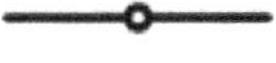

7

THE ARTS AND PRISONS

This chapter draws on the recent experiences of two musicians working in two very different prisons – Michael Goodey as Musician-in-Residence at HMP Wormwood Scrubs in London and Evi Nakou, at the time of writing Head of Learning and Participation, Greek National Opera, working at Korydallos Prison in Athens.

MUSICIAN-IN-RESIDENCE, HMP WORMWOOD SCRUBS

Michael Goodey is working on behalf of The Irene Taylor Trust, the Artistic Director of which, Sara Lee, has had a long association with Wormwood Scrubs going back to 1984. Reflecting on the quality of the work of the Trust in 2010, Sara commented:

> *One of the main reasons Music in Prisons projects have a high success rate is due to the continued emphasis on quality rather than quantity. In a time where getting value for money often means getting as many people as possible in a room in one go, we are fortunate that people realise and accept that the impact of a project on an*

individual is far more meaningful and long-lasting because of the quality of the experience.

Many factors are crucial in achieving and maintaining this quality and it is how these things combine that make the work so effective. The project team is one of the most important factors in its success. First and foremost, they are all amazing musicians but very importantly, each of them has the specific social skills needed to work with sometimes challenging prisoners and the patience to deal appropriately with the vagaries of the prison system. The core team has been working together regularly for many years and because of this, has been able to develop an enviable working relationship built on trust, support and a strong musical understanding. Having a team that is secure in its function means a positive and high-quality experience will be delivered to the participant group every time. It is the sensitive and enthusiastic approach of the project team which leads to such dramatic and positive responses from participants and this firstly enables the creation of music of the highest quality and secondly offers them an experience that will have a positive influence on their futures.
(See Renshaw, 2010, p.210)

Since this was written The Irene Taylor Trust has continued to build up its work in prisons, but it has also developed its rehabilitation programme, Sounding Out, for former prisoners and its Making Tracks and Young Producers programmes discussed in Chapters 4, 5 and 9. Within the prison system one significant development has been establishing Musician-in-Residence programmes in a number of prisons – HMP Coldingley, HMP Wakefield, HMP Spring Hill, HMP Highpoint, HMP Wandsworth, HMP Risley and HMP Wormwood Scrubs. The challenging work of these musicians-in-residence is described by Michael Goodey from his perspective in Wormwood Scrubs.

Testimony by Michael Goodey, Musician-in-Residence, HMP Wormwood Scrubs

I've been Musician-in-Residence at HMP Wormwood Scrubs for just over three years. It is a large Category B men's prison for those on remand or on short sentences, usually up to one year. It holds around 1,200 men and runs on a skeleton crew of officers. The role of Musician-in-Residence means I am at the prison every week and get a huge insight into a largely hidden and often misrepresented world. I observe the men I work with, the community and the politics of prison adjust and evolve in a very institutionalised microcosm.

People often ask what working in prison is like and I describe it as being brilliant, awful, tragic, hilarious, desperate, dysfunctional and joyous all at the same time. It is certainly eye-opening. Chronic under-funding and a lack of experienced staff make it a barely functioning institution. The Scrubs is a Victorian building and the wings have changed very little in one hundred and fifty years. The physical environment is oppressive: Everything is too loud and there is a constant background smell of drains and smoke. The sounds of iron gates clashing, doors slamming, dogs barking, alarm bells ringing, people screaming and shouting are ever present. There are rats and feral cats in the perpetually filthy grounds and drug use, violence and self-harm are constant. Ambulances and police cars are a regular sight.

After I've picked up my keys, unlocked and locked 15 doors and gates on my route through what I've just described, I'm in the Seacole Centre, where mental health outpatients come for appointments and groups. Twice a week I work with a group of anything from four to twelve men, with a massive diversity of life stories, musical tastes and experiences. The music group has had the highest attendance of any group at the Seacole Centre since it started. I'm told by members of the mental health team that it has had a direct impact on reduction of anxiety, self-harm, suicidal thoughts and improvement in engagement. I am often asked if I'm a music therapist, and am often referred to as one. I have to remind the people I work with that I am not a therapist and that I have never had any mental health training. Everything I know comes from experience. What I do know, I do not see through a clinical lens. I have to have conversations that include clinical language and discuss measurable outcomes but my practice is definitely not clinical. The group may well have clinical impacts but it is simply a jamming session. I work with men with a whole range of mental health problems including anxiety, PTSD, Schizophrenia and depression. The work is brilliant and I honestly forget where I am when the music is happening. When a session is at its best, it's just a room full of blokes making music together. It's that simple. Feedback from men who come to the group has included (word for word):

> "I swear, when I shut my eyes I leave this room."
> "I forget I'm in prison when I come here."
> "I've never felt this alive."
> "This is the only thing getting me through this."

The most common bit of written feedback, under the heading "Is there anything else you would like to add?" is "More sessions please". Sometimes, guys in the group will sit and listen with their eyes closed or go and stand in a narrow ray of light coming through one of the two five-centimetre open windows. They will often comment that they can now go back to the wings happy, less stressed and with a sense of achievement. Nine out of ten sessions are like this and can honestly be transcendental for those who take part. The sense "of leaving the room" can be very clear and immediate. What could be more therapeutic than that? Every now and again a session can be a bit mundane, unproductive or disruptive and I leave feeling relieved that it's over. It doesn't happen often.

I wouldn't claim that the work I do is life-changing for everyone who experiences it. But I do know for a fact that it has been the single thing that has supported some men through the most difficult time in their lives. Peer support and encouragement are big things. Even the slightest achievement in an individual or in the group as a whole is always noted and applauded by the group. There is also a genuine desire to be helpful, whether that's setting up and packing away, teaching each other parts, making the coffee or doing the washing up.

Making music together is undeniably special. In a world that is increasingly focused on individualism, acquisition of material wealth at any cost and at the detriment of relationships, our own well-being and the environment, there are few things left to be enjoyed in the moment and that bond us as equals. It feels so rare to be part of something that is only about the thing itself, where the goal of the activity is the activity. There is a lot of trust within the group. Fear of failure disappears very quickly and there is an almost child-like joy in being able to contribute to making original music and learning how to play an instrument. I see men unwind, let their guard down and communicate in an open and honest way. I feel very privileged to have the opportunity to run the group. I've learnt an indescribable amount about life, relationships, determination and fear. I've also learnt more about being in bands than I have from being in bands. (...)

(...) The men I work with are generally about my age, from London and many of them are big music fans. Many of us grew up listening to the same stuff. I don't feel like an expert in this environment. I feel connected to the wider context of their music and their lives - I've had friends go to prison and known many people with the same kind of chaos and darkness that often appears in the lives of prisoners. The music, swearing, talk about drugs and the slang all feel very familiar to me (the slang less so as I get older, the swearing more so). I am lucky to work, semi-officially, within a team of fantastic people who are passionate and ambitious. I feel autonomous, trusted and have a strong sense of belonging. The mental health team are predominantly women and none of the men are from London. My connection to the mental health team is based on values, beliefs and the shared experience of trying to achieve something we all understand in a difficult environment. Most of the time, my connection to the men I work with is much more tribal.

In my fifteen years of work, sometimes I've felt like I'm making music with people and sometimes at them. The balance varies from job to job, from project to project, depending on who I'm working with, the purpose of the project, funders' demands etc. Working in prison is the most inside of my work I've ever felt and that is still the case despite not sharing any personal information. They know nothing about my life and I know very little about their lives. We talk about music, films, food, the state of the world, the banality of "reality TV", social media and its negative impact on young people and all kinds of other stuff. Conversations can be deeply philosophical, insightful, touching, scary, funny, meandering or any combination of these. Observations and opinions can be very astute when you're so heavily controlled and when you may spend up to 23 hours a day in a cell.

The purpose of this piece was to describe what I do, why I do it, why and how I think engagement in the arts can make a qualitative difference to people's lives. You've had some detail but what I've included only scratches the surface of the world I work in. I could go on forever but was reminded while writing this that somebody else has already explained it much better than I have.

I love reading the feedback forms that get filled out every few weeks by participants. The comment that will stay with me the most was from a prisoner who barely spoke when he first attended the group and had never played an instrument before. His life story was tragic - he'd been particularly violently abused by his parents throughout his childhood, was bullied at school, consoled himself with alcohol and struggled to make friends. He was in prison for a crime that was essentially a major act of self-harm and had never hurt anyone. He was not angry or vengeful and just seemed very sad. He started playing the bass and stayed on it for about eight months. He gradually opened up and by the time he left he was teaching his parts to other people, and helping them by explaining song structures and so on. In one short sentence he perfectly summed up the purpose and potential impact of the group:

"In this group I am made to feel useful and wanted".

Well, so am I.

This could not be a stronger statement about why engaging in music-making in prison can be such a life-enhancing experience for all concerned, including the musician(s) leading the group. To describe this experience as "transcendental" just illustrates the value and significance of this kind of creative work. It has the potential to be life-changing at a very deep level and Michael Goodey captures this spirit so simply, yet vividly. But Michael's modesty plays down the qualities he brings to such musical and human encounters. Wide-ranging musical skills and cultural references have to be underpinned by those values and beliefs that resonate with people whose lives are almost seen as 'on hold'. It is as if the whole musical and social experience is bound together by a common humanity based on mutual respect. A feeling captured so well by the prisoner who said: "in this group I am made to feel useful and wanted". A similar sentiment also echoed by Michael.

PROJECT IN KORYDALLAS PRISON, ATHENS

Evi Nakou (Former Head of Learning and Participation, Greek National Opera) presents a collective testimony, *The Redbreast Robin*, which includes a statement about the Korydallos Prison in

Athens for male political activists by Andreas-Dimitris Bourzoukos and a poem by Tasos Theofilou, both of whom she encountered whilst working in the prison. Evi prefaces her shared testimony with reference to Margaret Atwood's book on *Freedom* (Atwood, 2018).

———o———

Collective Testimony by Evi Nakou with Andreas-Dimitris Bourzoukous and poetry by Tasos Theofilou

The Redbreast Robin (Margaret Atwood)
'A robin redbreast in a cage, puts all Heaven in a rage'
(William Blake).

The robin redbreast is safer in the cage: it won't get eaten by cats or smash into windows. It will have lots to eat. But it will also not be able to fly wherever he likes. Presumably this is what troubles the inhabitants of heaven: they object to the restriction placed on the flight options of a fellow winged being. The robin should live in nature, where it belongs; it should have 'freedom to', the active mode, rather than 'freedom from', the passive mode
('We are Double-Plus Unfree' by Margaret Atwood)

In March 2017 a group of 19 male prisoners allowed themselves the freedom to perform a 40 minutes long music concert in front of an audience of professional musicians, prison guards, journalists, judges, policemen as well as other prisoners. The music concert was the culmination of a two-months creative process of music-making through improvisation and group composition. With the exception of a handful of amateur musicians, the rest of the participants had never been engaged in a music-making process, let alone had they ever attempted to play a musical instrument.

The concert consisted of seven original compositions, some of which included spoken poetry whereas others were instrumental. What ended up being the band for this concert, was a music community that was formed during weekly workshops and facilitated by four female artists/workshop leaders – myself, MC Harper, Eva Karterou and Thalia Marie Papadopoulou – for a period of two months. As this was the first music-making project taking place in a correctional facility in Greece, the project ended up being the biggest learning curve that I have experienced throughout my practice to this day, at both an artistic as well as managerial level.

About Korydallos Prison: A testimony within a testimony
Andreas-Dimitrios Bourzoukos

A prison could not but be a miniature of the very society that 'maintains' its existence. And while theoretically one would expect that imprisoned people would create a community as a reflex to oppression and capitalism, once again, it imposes the dominance of the individual versus the collective.

Bringing promises of reformation to the correctional system of Greece and the construction standards of prisons in Greece, Korydallos Prison was widely advertised since the very first day of its construction in 1961 in Korydallos, a semi-urban neighborhood on the outskirts of Athens. The initial planning for the design of the prison's facilities capitalised on cells whose amenities wouldn't differ much from those of a hotel room. Needless to mention that due to the overpopulation of the prison from its early days back in 1967, those comforts were never offered to the stakeholders. The prison was intended to host 600 prisoners divided into six wings, but since its population exceeded by far the initial expectations, each cell ended up 'hosting' up to four or five people, whilst the prison population at Korydallos comprised 3000 imprisoned people. It comes as no surprise that hygiene rules and living standards were and still remain unacceptable, while cleanliness is left to the initiative of the imprisoned themselves.

Another crucial aspect of the operation of Korydallos Prison is the management of the imprisoned by command and control. Over a long period of time Korydallos Prison has experienced numerous upheavals, uprisings and various kinds of tensions that were dealt with through the exercise of repression by the prison's administration. Inevitably, instead of introducing stability, repression generated additional tensions and functioned as a means of uniting the imprisoned against the administration. Such an explosive mixture being created inside a prison that hosts thousands of people within its urban fabric, can become extremely dangerous for the prison guards, the correctional system and the state itself. Following the '90s, when uprisings, escapes, beatings and torture amongst other things led to chaos within the prison, it was apparent that control and repression would only be possible through drug trafficking.

Large quantities of drugs were 'allowed' into prisons, heroin being the most popular, with the aim of aborting the momentum and the dynamics of the individuals and communities of the imprisoned people. Beyond its direct objective of control, such a tactic introduced immense profits to those involved in these transactions, precisely because of the large population of the prison. Korydallos' Prison anthropogeography introduces a large diversity, due to its judicial nature as a prison. It therefore comes by definition that since the opportunities for artistic expression are to a large extent exhausted, the initiative of the imprisoned in areas like painting, improvised handicrafts and occasionally in music, and their creativity couldn't flourish due to the lack of consistent support by professional artists/facilitators.

Bearing in mind these words of anarchist Andreas-Dimitrios Bourzoukos, a prisoner at that time and participant in our music workshop, I as an artist and co-leader of this project, had to rethink about the power relations within the group, the roles I was taking as well as the language I was using in this particular context. Overall, the music ended up being a means to either a personal or a collective end; a vehicle for self-expression and stress-release as well as a drive for creating a hybrid community within the prison.

Having deprivation of freedom as the fundamental factor of the given context, I could only feel honest to the people I was working with, both participants and co-leaders, if I were to eliminate any power-relationships and the dipole of leader-participant. Throughout the process, my main goal was to co-create new music and text of high quality with a group of collaborators that were treated on equal terms. My role was to share and not to uphold my music knowledge, and to provide the group with social and musical skills that would empower them to translate their thoughts into sound and music. Co-operative listening and improvising were key elements in the process. Decision-making, either about the music itself or for the practicalities of our public performances, was made after hours-long conversations with the group.

Those conversations led to a realisation that has subsequently influenced my practice and thinking as a political subject. Even though the prisoners were from their beginning linked to a larger project of transformation of individuals, the creative process and the artistic outcome needed to aim for the transformation of the attitude of society towards imprisoned people. Within the context of a music concert that takes place in a prison, both the performers and the audience are challenged to reflect on issues of ownership, authority and inclusion.

Looking at the larger picture, music-making projects in the community are constituted in and by the subjectivities they allow as well as those they disallow. It is the very figure of the enabler of a music-making process that presents itself as the scholar that upholds the authority and excellence in the field. There is always the danger that the enabler could disguise this process well, under the veneer of a proclaimed participatory artistic process, in which artistic potentialities are nevertheless silenced and erased.

As a female, white middle class individual, born in Southern Europe in the late '80s, accessibility to arts education was something that I always took for granted: a process within which I could understand culture, history and politics, and therefore the world that surrounds me. Music to me has always been a tool, a means to non-verbal expression and communication, and therefore a way to feel a sense of belonging in existing communities. When finding myself estranged from those communities, I would immediately look for possibilities of co-shaping new communities with other individuals. Looking at my practice as an artist, I find myself highly engaged in a creative process only when it has the potential to encourage heterogeneity in relation to class, culture and gender, as well as ideally to provoke change in the artistic and societal landscape in which we live and work.

It is that safe space that I expect myself to 'hold' in my practice, which has the qualities to encourage individuals to harness their intellect and affects equally through the arts. As a performing artist and workshop leader, I aspire to a political practice in which individuals are voicing their multifaceted and shifting selves, and encourage a conscious process of rewriting of the 'self' in relation to a new understanding of history, culture and community.

23.10.2012
by Tasos Theofilou

One day it will all be over.
And we'll say that we tried at least.
That we didn't come to life for nothing
That we haven't burdened the earth for nothing.
That we left something behind.

And our faces will be wrinkled.
One wrinkle for every cut.
For every moment of despair.
For every moment of eternal loneliness.

Those who fear their wrinkles
Fear their past
Their futile present
Their foretold future.
They hate themselves and what they become.

Time leaves its marks.
And we'll bear them with pride.

Since January 2017, the Learning and Participation Department of the Greek National Opera has been facilitating the music workshop in Korydallos Male Prison on a weekly basis. In April 2017 the band, with its initial formation, recorded four out of seven original compositions that were given in the form of a CD album to the families of the participants. In June 2017, the original band with the addition of new members composed and performed an original score for the theatrical play *The Tempest* by William Shakespeare, which was performed in Korydallos Prison by prisoners. In July 2018 the band, with its new formation, performed four original compositions in a concert dedicated specifically to an audience of prisoners and to family members, and which also included a choreographed piece of hip-hop dance performed by a prisoner.

Evi's collective testimony demonstrates her deep commitment to collaborative creative processes and to fostering a sense of shared responsibility in all her work. In many ways she offers a political as well as a moral and artistic statement. For Evi there is no place for 'artistic ego' or assumed 'artistic authority'.

Everything hangs on the music leaders making meaningful and respectful connections to the context, to each individual voice and to that of the collective. With the emphasis on co-creation through improvisation, co-operative listening and shared decision-making, this process challenges all participants and audience to "reflect on issues of ownership, authority and inclusion" – issues that are very pertinent in the world outside prison at the moment. What stands out is that Evi is evolving a philosophy of action, a 'political practice', which is underpinned by a commitment to diversity regarding social class, culture and gender, together with a determination to provoke social and artistic change – a major challenge to individual artists, cultural organisations and to society as a whole.

8

THE ARTS, REFUGEES AND MIGRANTS

This chapter focuses on four arts projects with refugees and migrants: a collaboration between The Irene Taylor Trust, the Royal Philharmonic Orchestra (RPO) Resound and Praxis Community Projects in London; Sounds of Change working with Palestinian refugees for NGO Ruwwad in Jordan; a group of musicians from London working in collaboration with Greek National Opera in Melissa, a community centre for migrant women in central Athens; and the work of Osnat Ritter, an educator and activist from Israel/Palestine and Founder of Tachles Art Centre for Palestinian and Israeli youth in Haifa.

These four case studies – the Lullaby Project, Sounds of Change, Melissa and Osnat's story – illustrate vividly and sensitively what can be achieved by artists who have the values, skills and attitudes to make a qualitative difference to people's lives. What stands out as a constant thread, both in this chapter and in those concerned with mental health, prisons and education, is the strength of motivation and integrity of people who have a deep belief in what they do really matters. For them, addressing social issues through engaging in the arts is a sine qua non. There is no place for self-absorption. Inner strength, yes, but always focused on others – on strangers, on other communities, on other contexts. As was touched on in Chapter 5, a synergy between the inner and the outer, between the artist's creative voice and his or her sensibility to social needs, is the motor that lies at the heart of socially engaged creative practice.

THE LULLABY PROJECT, THE IRENE TAYLOR TRUST, RPO AND PRAXIS COMMUNITY PROJECTS

In summer 2017 The Irene Taylor Trust (ITT) brought the Lullaby Project (originally developed by Carnegie Hall's Weill Music Institute and previously delivered by ITT in collaboration with the Chicago Symphony Orchestra Civic Fellows in Chicago) to the UK, in partnership with the RPO Resound. The project supported fathers in prison, and refugee and migrant mothers from Praxis Community Projects WINGS group to write original lullabies for their young children, aiming to enhance the bond between parent and child, with very powerful moving results. The project was supported by Arts Council England, Lucille Graham Trust and Swan Mountain Trust. An independent researcher, Sara Ascenso, published her evaluation of the project, *The Lullaby Project: Areas of Change and Mechanisms of Impact*, in November 2017.[15]

Writing in the 2017 Praxis Impact Report Sally Daghlian, Chief Executive, emphasises the importance of adopting a holistic approach when working with migrants. Commenting on the success of the Lullaby Project she says:

> *The moving lyrics reflected the universal feelings of love, hope, passion and pride of a mother for her child, expressed in unique and distinct ways. This project exemplifies our holistic approach – whilst providing vital*

---

[15] www.irenetaylortrust.com/what-we-do/our-projects/special-projects/lullaby/

> *help with accommodation, support and legal advice, we*
> *also bring people together to find a sense of belonging*
> *and inner strength, and to help them to thrive despite*
> *their precarious circumstances.*
> Praxis Impact Report, 2017, p.2. [16]

After the Lullaby Project I had the privilege of having a conversation with two mothers, Maria and Moussumi, and Emma Gardiner, Group Work Coordinator of Praxis. Not surprisingly, the complexities and inequities of immigration were a major issue, and for people like Maria and Moussumi the understanding and support of the WINGS group is a lifeline. During their weekly sessions everyone is free to share their problems knowing that they will not be judged. WINGS is seen as more like a family, thriving on its mutual trust and openness.

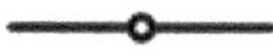

Testimonies by Maria and Moussumi, Participants in the Lullaby Project

Maria: "At the moment I am navigating in the sea and I don't know where the flow of water is taking me. I am upset about the immigration situation that my kids and I are facing. It's scary, it's giving me high blood pressure and anxiety.
I had dreams (I still have dreams) and I wonder if one day I will realise them but sadly I am getting older and not achieving anything. Just eating, thinking. I take my older son to school and after school club. I push myself to do some activities with my little son too.
When will this immigration issue come to an end? It's amazing how someone's life can depend on just one document. When will I be free to travel and work and study? People don't know that having immigration problems when you have kids is not at all a joking matter. You can't do anything. I am getting old without

---

really achieving anything in my life. I am only able to give all that I can to my children.

The Lullaby Project was great and fun for me. Making music out of what I feel and to see someone singing for me was something I will never forget. It was very emotional to hear other mums' lyrics – that was so touching. When I am an old granny I will listen to the lullabies we wrote and it will bring me memories of yesterday. "

Moussumi: "I felt good about it. I can tell my children what's going on in this world. When they listen to the song, they're quiet and hug me. Sometime I just cry whilst my children are listening and dancing. But my song is a little sad, and my children are quiet when they're listening. The Lullaby Project was very good. The musicians came and talked to us, showing us some words and I started crying. The sound of the words and what they said, as a Mum, was very personal. Every night I play the song on my mobile and the children listen and go to sleep."

Further responses from the Evaluation of the Lullaby Project:
Areas of change and mechanisms of impact (Sara Ascenco, 2017)

Fatimah: "This project gave me confidence. From the beginning, I had no idea about music and didn't know how what we discussed would change to music. [...] When it was recorded and I listened to it at home, I felt that I had given something from the inside to my children and I was very happy." (ibid., p.26)

The Evaluation Report also emphasises the important link between the mothers' experience of achievement and the strong sense of meaning gained from creating their lullabies. This stood out as "a landmark for their resilience and a reminder of both their process of struggle and the hope they maintain". (ibid., p.27)

Ella: *"[felt her children] will listen to it in the future, when our problems will be solved. Ah, then everything will be okay.*

Listening back to this music, we'll be like: "wow … so, this is where I came from", you know? This is the step I went through … And our children, as well, when they listen to that, they will know how much suffering mummy went through." (ibid., p.27)

The Evaluation also highlighted the 'bonding effect' of engaging with the creative process. "Besides promoting a greater sense of connectedness [between the mothers and their] babies, the lullabies also functioned as a means for deepening the bond among the mothers themselves, especially in the case of a sub-group who share the same house. They recorded each other's songs and sung them regularly to one another and to each other's children" (ibid., p.29).

Sophia: *"It helps in our connection a lot. Because with this lullaby, first I was using only his name when I sang to him, but now it's some words that come from my heart with the sound that I always make with his name … Yeah. My other son, David wasn't there, but I'm sure when he will listen, he will feel… he will recognise that."* (ibid., p.29)

Ella: *"And we know which song we should sing to our children, like, I mean, Preetha's song … I'm very close to her, so her song touched me. Seriously, I think it's the lady that helped her to blend those words. She did a fantastic job because, as a person who knows Preetha, when she starts singing, I feel … every word, I feel them inside me. I cried that day. So, when I see [Preetha's children], I always sing that song for them. And she sings my song to my children."* (ibid. pp. 29-30)

One of the most significant findings from the Evaluation was that the Lullaby Project led to "enhanced reflection" in all the participants.

> *For the group of mothers, this theme was mentioned in relation with the development of a richer perspective about their life, implying gratitude and hope. The*

reflection about their story and the narrative of their relationship with their child, brought insight on what they have received since coming to the UK and on their own sense of resilience, strengthening hope and optimism about future goals. (ibid., p.32)

The person responsible for the WINGS group of mothers involved in the Lullaby Project was Emma Gardiner, whose testimony helps to provide an informed understanding of the context in which Praxis works.

———◇———

Testimony by Emma Gardiner, Group Work Coordinator of Praxis

I am sure that there are those better placed than I am to talk at length about the positive impact music has on young people, and the transformative effects taking part in creative projects can (and very often) have. What I can reflect on, though, is the context within which such projects take place. I work with migrants in East London, delivering community work at an organisation called Praxis Community Projects. Although my observations have been shaped by working with this group, I believe that they hold true for people more generally – those who access services, but also for me, for you, probably.

Much of our society, and most definitely the third sector, takes its shape through categorising people; sometimes based on age, sometimes gender, sometimes race, sometimes vulnerability, sometimes trauma, sometimes type of trauma, sometimes disability, sometimes income threshold; categories that are discrete and rigid. This has shaped, and simplified, our understanding of what a person is – you are old, or you are young. You are homeless, or you are housed. You are vulnerable, or you are not vulnerable. You cannot be both. It is not compatible within this framework to, for example, one day be performing a poem about your life to 100 people, and the next be unable to get out of bed. And yet clearly we understand this to be false, so why do we buy into it for those with whom we work? People are, innately, good and bad. They are happy and they are sad. They are weak and they are strong. Yes, we perpetuate this falsehood – through the delineation of our work, through funder strategies, applications, reports, research, and more broadly through allocation of local services, benefits systems, data collection, stories, journalism – all organising our reality using the same set of rules – if you are this, you cannot be that.

It is this framework that restricts our ability to measure change – we are led to believe that successful work means people neatly travelling in a straight line, from one end of a scale to another – building resilience, improving self-esteem, gaining skills and knowledge. Expectations for young people within this framework can be terrifyingly high – I often ask myself, would I expect this of myself? Of the people in my own life? When we transpose these notions onto ourselves instead of those 'in need' they often seem unachievably ambitious. We have othered those we work with, categorised them as fundamentally different to us, and so are not in the habit of making this comparison. We expect the people we work with to go from a place of vulnerability to becoming self-confident, 'resilient', no longer co-dependent and able to deal with life's challenges within the lifetime of a project, and because of that project.

This framework also requires a world view centred on the individual, within which change happens at the individual level, often in isolation from other people. In my work I encounter people who have a different world view, a different understanding of the self, and its relationship with the other. Often people I work with struggle to engage and benefit from western models of psychotherapy, because they are shaped on notions of the self, the individual, not on the village, the community.

Because the language we use to talk about change (resilience, self-esteem, self-worth, wellbeing) is geared towards the individual, we can fall into the trap of assigning responsibility of someone's issues to themselves – i.e., in order to deal with the challenges you face, you need to become more resilient, or you need to stop drinking, you need to get therapy and improve your mental health. But what about if the reason you can't speak up for yourself, you are an addict, or are depressed, is because you have been waiting for three years for the Home Office to make a decision on your asylum case? Or because you experience racism on an almost daily basis – on the street, in shops, in newspapers? Or because you no longer have a community? Because you cannot share your meals with your family? Because you are not allowed to work, to volunteer, to move forward with your life? Let's transpose this onto our own lives; if you were experiencing all this, and someone says to you, 'perhaps you need to become more resilient', what would you think? We maintain the status quo and allocate responsibility to the individual to improve their own lives, not to government, social systems, education; things that, in truth, are the root cause of the issues experienced by most people.

Within this context, though, sometimes we do see positive change in people – through helping them to challenge the structures that oppress them, through creating spaces within which they are able to be in control, to rebuild some of what society has taken from them – equality, purpose, relationships, community, access to justice. It's long, slow work. Changes are often small, and unexpected. They often don't look the way we expect them to, either. A positive outcome, to me, is when people taught to always be grateful start complaining. Or when a group of women who meet every week sync their periods. Or when a young woman turns up to a group without makeup on for the first time.

——o——

Emma's insights, based on considerable experience, invite us to see the world of the migrant, or the world of the 'other' in a qualitatively different way, through a lens that challenges many of our well-worn assumptions. One of her perceptive observations echoes those of Daisy Swift in Chapter 5, who is writing in a totally different context. But there are important parallels. The framework outlined by Emma presupposes a world view premised on the primacy of the individual, whereas many migrants have a view of self that is more rooted in the community or the collective. In her critique of the perceived "hierarchy of musical excellence" in the music profession, Daisy comments that there is a status differential between genres and careers in an industry that places individual success at the pinnacle of a pyramid of achievement. For Daisy "this approach to music-making is deeply problematic; its individual rather than relational approach stands in stark opposition to the collaborative spirit that makes music so powerful, so important".

The emphasis on the 'relational' and the 'collective voice' advocated by both Daisy and Emma lies at the heart of the creative collaborative process used by many performing artists responding to people's different needs in community contexts. This stood out clearly in the case of the Lullaby Project, the success of which was dependent on using collaborative processes that were responsive to the human needs of the migrant mothers and their children.

SOUNDS OF CHANGE: WORKING WITH PALESTINIAN REFUGEES FOR RUWWAD IN JORDAN

The music organisation Sounds of Change was founded in The Netherlands by Lucas Dols in June 2017. He was soon joined by Maite van der Marel, who has written the following testimony. They work in and around conflict areas to empower people through music, especially in Jordan, Palestine, Lebanon and Egypt. They believe the world needs strong community builders in order to foster social change and they see that engaging in the arts is a powerful tool in building these positive role models. At the moment their focus is largely on volunteers, students, teachers, aid workers and musicians – people who want to reach out to other people, who work within the Syrian or Palestinian refugee camps, or within the educational field. They help them to strengthen their own qualities and skills and enrich them with a more flexible mind-set. They bring out their stories through music and help them in building skills to respond to the needs of their environment.

Reflecting on her recent experiences with Sounds of Change, Maite confronts us with her honesty: "You can imagine that my perspective on the world has sharpened through my work in the often conservative and torn Middle East. To be honest, being closer to problematic, inhumane and devastating situations leaves me more puzzled than ever. I understand less and less of this world. But I'm determined to put my values into practice and I try to align what is right with what is possible. I am a pragmatic idealist". Maite's testimony takes us straight into the work of Sounds of Change with Palestinian refugees for NGO Ruwwad Jordan, a community development organisation focusing on the education of children, the empowerment of women and skills building for young people.

———o———

Testimony by Maite van der Marel, musician, Sounds of Change

I – Dreams

Make your dream come true
Be different in any way

No one can judge you
We all love you this way

Hand in hand with our values
We enrich our society
We walk the hard road
We walk the whole road

To build our country
To make the dreams come true

Your differences complement us
And the music enriches us

("Ruwwad song" – lyrics written by Sounds of Change trainees in Amman, Jordan)

As a child I was also a dreamer.
Unlike these young people, I didn't grow up in an environment with conflict or war. But through working in these areas, I found out that even though we are from different cultures, we share the same needs.

Our most fundamental needs are safety, food, shelter and love. But there are also needs that people might not be aware of having, causing a destructive effect on their lives when they are not being met, like depression, social exclusion or conflict. I am talking about needs like identity, freedom and creation. Meeting these needs brings a sense of belonging, the feeling of being accepted; the feeling of autonomy and the self-esteem to follow your passion, and the ability to use the power of your imagination. Meeting these needs for myself has also brought me a lot personally. It has helped to change the way I perceive myself and the way I live my values.

Imagine what a creative mind-set, leadership skills and sense of autonomy could bring you, when living in a war zone, being stuck in a refugee camp or living in a marginalised area and growing up with a very conservative religion? In the work I do with Sounds of

Change I want our participants to discover what they can achieve by meeting their needs, and for them to see how music can help to transform their lives.

[In my testimony] I will take you with me to the worlds I've immersed myself in most recently and draw on the stories and experiences of the people I worked with.

II – Pioneering

We miss you, sea
We miss you, sea
You have been deprived from our visit
I swear it's only because of the checkpoints
That you have been deprived from seeing us

To those who live near you, lucky them
Because they see your waves

We miss you sea
We miss you sea
You have been deprived from our visit

Under the pineapple tree we sit
We sing for our country, and sit on the swing
We've found our ancestors, we're so happy
We sing for our country, hoping to be young again
To be young again (6x)

('Nostalgia' – lyrics written by Sounds of Change trainees in Bethlehem, Palestine)

Facing an intimidating 8-meter-high separation wall halts my breath. On one side of the wall I see prosperity, on the other a distinctly less rosy reality; the Palestinian reality. These people live in a country that is not recognised by all countries in the world, and they don't have the same human rights as us. They're not able to freely move. The army frequently invades houses in the middle of the night. People live with daily fear, violence and shootings. More and more land is taken by the Israeli settlers.

The lyrics above reflect this Palestinian life in a very touching way. The women we created this song with, speak straight from the heart. They see, smell and hear the sea, but they can't reach it because of the wall. They face humiliations daily, for example at the checkpoints which takes hours to pass through. Their voices are muted. But they sing for their country. The lyrics as well as the melody of the song are so strong. Feeling the power of these women in these writing sessions is incredible.

I realise how much freedom I have as a Dutch citizen. 'Dutchies' are welcome anywhere in the world. Also within my country I'm very free: I can say what I want, dress how I want. I can be stubborn, idealistic and withdraw myself from the mainstream, and still be accepted. I am independent and have an economically stable situation. I have the freedom to follow my heart, to make music, and to travel the world.

Unfortunately, some governments limit the freedom of groups of people. The political game often seems cruel and standing up against it feels like fighting a losing battle. I know we won't be able to change these political outcomes with our music programme, but within these contexts I want to focus on bringing back humanity, and to show people a different example. Art has the power to break through the sometimes-thick walls of darkness that people experience, and reach to the heart. It creates a new colour palette to draw with. All the colours are already there; we just help to release them. With this they can be part of a change within their circle of influence.

I truly believe young people are part of the solution in these conflicted areas. Unfortunately, most of them are excluded from their society by their own government. They are not being listened to. They are not being seen. But they have a lot to say and we need to hear them. Our partner organisation 'Ruwwad', which means 'pioneers', also believes in the power of the youth. They are based in Jordan, Lebanon, Egypt and Palestine, often in very challenging areas, to change the community from within.

Ruwwad is a non-profit community development organisation that works with disenfranchised and marginalised communities through education and youth volunteerism. The youth volunteers are being offered scholarships to study and in return they serve the community with teaching children voluntarily. Their core focus is embracing diversity. They have ongoing conversations with the community to meet their needs. For their youth volunteers they provide open discussions, reflection and counselling sessions, and they work with them on personal growth. I'm impressed with how they break through stigmas and create opportunities together with these young people. They help them to change from having a throwing-stones-perspective, to pro-active citizens with an I-take-responsibility-perspective.

III –The Jungle

We also work with Ruwwad in Jordan. What I learned is that every country in the Middle East has its own characteristics, its own issues and even from city to city the dynamic can be different, because all people have different beliefs and backgrounds. It's the diversity that makes a country, city or neighbourhood so rich and colourful.

Jordan is one of the few countries in peace in the Middle East and at first sight feels pretty easy-going. Yet we enter places where the situation is not always that peaceful. Upcoming extremism and increased violence is becoming every day's business.

"Welcome to the jungle", Hamzeh says, when we enter the Palestinian Camp in East-Amman. Hamzeh is one of our trainees – a young healthy looking guy that usually smiles a lot. He invited us for dinner at his art studio. Hamzeh studies Fine Arts, which is

very uncommon in this neighbourhood. He takes us deeper and deeper into the camp. Prayer time has just finished, so the streets are crowded with people of all ages. They stare at us; we're strangers. There's a lot of garbage, and street cats seem to take over the area. We move in between the houses that are built very close together, higher and higher up the hill through the narrow streets, until we reach Hamzeh's place. Walls full of sketches, an easel with unfinished work and the smell of paint. His studio feels like an oasis of peace and creativity within the jungle.

After he has shown his work and experiments there's one thing that strikes me. In most of the paintings, people either don't have a face or they show their back. He explains us his frustration about people blindly following the rules of Islam, how difficult it is to have your own identity, or to say what you think. How people criticise you when you choose a different way. I wonder if these paintings are a reflection of how he experiences his society. But it seems he has a lot of freedom within his family and he also feels free to experiment with painting more detailed faces. At the same time, he is fascinated by changing the identities of his images by not showing all the details. And most importantly, his family supports him in his journey, even though it is against the rules of their religion.

The next day we enter a beautiful cultural café in Amman, where we meet with Raghad, our 22-year old trainee from the same group. Her hair is covered with a hijab (scarf) and she usually wears a jilbab (long dress) with a striking colour. She always greets us with a big smile and warm hug. For Lucas a 'virtual hug': a hug with a little distance.

She speaks with a soft but clear voice and explains:
> *"In our religion it is a taboo to paint people's faces, to draw, to act in theatre, and also to mix with boys. You cannot do it. I always have discussions with my father. He understands me sometimes. Within our discussions I try to explain to him that when I was exposed to guys, I*

became very aware of what I want. In our society girls are born to grow up, marry and be a housekeeper, nothing else. I tried to explain to him how my mind has changed. I do not want just that, I want to make my dreams come true, to leave a footprint on my society. I don't want to be just a machine to grow children."

In the communities we work with, a lot of young people grow up in a very conservative environment, like Hamzeh and Raghad. Through what Raghad learned about herself, she is now determined to make a positive change. She is a very soft person, but with enormous strength. I'm curious how she images the footprint she would like to leave on her society. She says:

"I discovered myself in Ruwwad and found out who is Raghad, what I want to do and who I want to be. This gave me the courage to struggle and fight against my parents for my aims. If all of our children in the schools discover themselves, they will be very strong and they will build our community. That is what I'm aiming for. I want to be part of creating a healthy community. They have to stop judging women; they have to stop making borders for them and lies for them. They say you are born to do chores and bring children. Nothing else. You are not important."

This is how I believe engaging in the arts can make a difference. It means that through the process of expressing yourself, you start to explore and discover more and more. It opens a broader perspective. The important part in this process is not only to reflect on yourself, but also on others. What do you see around you? How do you feel about that? What does this teach you about yourself? How do you see the world? Within this reflective process, the opportunity to deconstruct and reconstruct your own framework and identity grows. This is a highly transformative process that can cause a true shift in the paradigm.

In some of the groups we work with in the Middle East, we find it hard to break through barriers that are a result of a conservative and war-torn society. Our trainees are sometimes not used to reach to their own emotions and ideas. Or to being asked their opinion, to invent a new idea. It's a process that takes a while and has to be handled with care. We can't just come in and expect people to be open, vulnerable and creative, when for some of them their environment has been very strict, close-minded or unsafe until this point. We need to invest a lot in creating a safe space, to respect people for who they are and slowly explore new openings and extend their boundaries together with them.

But all groups are different, and I am always surprised. When we started working with the Ruwwad group in Amman in August 2018, we were very touched by these young people and the process that unfolded. I loved the moment when we came to the point – I think it was the second day – of improvising together. We were sitting in a circle. Lucas played some chords on the ukulele, and sang some melodies we sang back to him. He slowly worked towards every single person to improvise like he had been doing. If it wasn't for Lucas's incredibly inspiring energy that usually influences people to follow, I wouldn't have dared to do this so early in the process. But what happened transcended every expectation. The power of the group in that very moment, creating and holding a safe space together in order for everyone to embrace their vulnerability and take the step to bring out their own voice, was a magical moment by which you could see people being elevated. They all took the responsibility for this process, even though expressing themselves in music was a big step in a new direction for most of them.

The next day Raghad came to us with a big smile. I could feel her excitement. On her way to us, an idea for a song came to her. She sang it to me straight from the heart. It touched me. The spark in her eyes, the pureness of this little creative burst; I took that energy with me the whole week and I think she influenced the whole group with it. The creative process was flowing so naturally all week. Now, in October, we looked back on this moment with her.

> *"I was feeling really happy, totally happy. There is no expression to say how I felt that day. And I will always keep singing this song. It also made me feel sad a little bit. I have very distinctive abilities, but the main people in my life don't give me the chance to prove them that I have these abilities. So I can't really show who I am."*

When I asked her what is so powerful about music or the arts, and why are they important in her society, she explained:

> *"I feel that this is a different way to express yourself. To make your inner feelings, the very hurtful feelings come out to the world in a beautiful way. They may be ugly feelings. But we can express them in a beautiful way. [...] So if there is no art, when there's no music, people will keep hurting each other, because they don't have another way to express their feelings and their heart emotions. The result of that is what you see now happening in the Arab world. There is war everywhere, people keep killing each other."*

She expressed the urgency of shifting the paradigm in her environment:

> *"People around me are living in the cage of illusion. They do not know what is happening in the world. As long as they don't take the step to face the world, or go to places like Ruwwad, to mix with people with different thoughts and different cultures, they will not find their way to get out of this cage."*

IV – Dreams come true

'Ahead of society'

We have to remind ourselves that a transformation process takes time. I also learned that I can have an opinion about a different culture, behaviour, belief or whatsoever from my own background, but I have to respect people's values and beliefs. I have to realise that they are always part of a community, different from my own. Even if they do things I don't believe in, even if they might be radicalising, they are still the brother of someone, or the daughter of someone. I need to respect this and therefore I want to work inside-out of the community. *"Things take the time they take"*, poet Mary Oliver says so beautifully.

But I do believe the arts have the function to be 'ahead of society' and my idealism cannot easily be broken. Look at the lyrics I started my testimony with. I believe these young people are ahead of their society and they will make a change. We have to keep involving young people in these creative processes, in order to open consciousness, ask questions and elevate the mind. We have to embrace the diversity of people all around the world and realise that even though we are from different cultures we share the same needs. We need to be hand-in-hand – not only to fulfil our dreams, but to make the sound of change together.

MELISSA: COMMUNITY CENTRE FOR MIGRANT WOMEN IN ATHENS

Maite's powerful testimony again reinforces the importance of the 'relational', the 'collective', the 'collaborative', the 'familial' when working in sensitive, human contexts. This principle is further developed in Detta Danford's testimony about the work of her ensemble, Breakfast Club, in Melissa, a community centre for migrant women in Athens. An added dimension to her reflections is that Detta sees their work in Melissa through the eyes of a woman and a recent mother. This further strengthens the feeling of the 'familial', the importance of respecting persons, which very much resonated with the women in the centre.

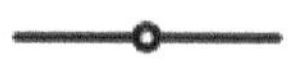

Testimony by Detta Danford,
musician and Guildhall School tutor

In May 2018, I was invited by my friend and colleague Evi Nakou to go to Athens to work with her on a project we had devised with our ensemble Breakfast Club, in partnership with the Greek National Opera, for which Evi at that time was Head of the Learning and Participation Department. To give a little more context, Breakfast Club (Evi Nakou, Rhia Parker, Natasha Zielazinski and myself) are a quartet of winds, strings and voice who play a fairly broad mix of music, including new and contemporary repertoire and early and renaissance music, alongside a mix of folk music and song. But more than this, we are four dear friends, who are drawn to making and playing music together despite the challenges of working with our instrumentation (which includes recorder, flutes of various kinds and 'cello - an unusual mix to say the least!)

In fact, the challenge of this combination has become part of the defining sound and approach of the ensemble, and in the five or so years we have been playing together we have found that we have enjoyed the challenge of selecting and arranging repertoire for ourselves (there is not much music written for this combination of instruments!) And, from the early days of scouring the Guildhall School Library looking for suitable open scores, we have developed a collaborative approach which involves each of us bringing ideas and suggestions for pieces that stem from our own individual interests and passions. This has led to a repertoire of music that includes folk songs and instrumental pieces from West Africa, Japan, America and England alongside music by the likes of Howard Skempton, Carlo Gesualdo, György Kurtág and Morton Feldman.

I love playing music with Breakfast Club Dand I can see that part of my love for this ensemble and what I cherish most about it, apart from the music we make together, is that it is deeply rooted in our friendship, support and love for each other. Many of our friends joke with us that the 'Club' part of Breakfast Club seems to far outweigh any of the other parts and indeed, rehearsals often start with at least an hour or more of catching up, chatting and finding out what has been happening in each other's lives, before any music-making actually starts to take place! And of course, it's not that we don't get down to some more serious, focused rehearsal when we meet, but over time, we have developed an approach to our meetings that makes much more space for our personal lives, struggles, issues and stories than other ensembles I've been a part of. On reflection, there are lots of practical reasons for this - that Evi lives far away in Athens and so it is important for us to take the time to catch up with her life in person when we see her, but also at this time in our lives, each of us has been going through their own important milestones, including marriage, pregnancy and birth!

When I think about the values we hold as an ensemble and about my own personal values, I also see that the placing of our personal friendships and connections as people at the heart of the ensemble is no accident, but rather a reflection of how all four of us live and what we adhere to in our work as musicians, teachers and creative music practitioners, where connecting as people first and foremost is our starting point. I also recognise and believe that within Breakfast Club this approach makes our music-making stronger and the work we do together more meaningful for us and for our audiences and those we work with. When we play together, we play from a place of joy, of trust and of deep care and love. I hope and believe that it will also make the ensemble more sustainable and more grounded, rooted and sure of itself in terms of what we are doing and why.

Over the last couple of years, alongside performing as an ensemble together, Evi has invited us twice to Athens to curate and lead projects based in the community. The first was in 2016, in a residential hospital called Asilo Aniaton, in which we were artists in residence for a week, working in a disused ward and creating three multi-disciplinary promenade performances for residents and the public that took place within the hospital grounds and in the local area around the hospital. The second took place this summer, at Melissa, a community centre for migrant women in central Athens. Both of these projects have had a huge impact on me as an artist and as a human being, and they are both experiences in which I have felt a profound celebration and coming together of my artistry and my human-ness – of what I hold most dear and of most value in my life and my work.

For the purposes of this writing, I will focus on the project we did in May 2018, working with the women at Melissa. For this project, we worked with a group of women who met regularly at Melissa and with a group of instrumentalists and singers who were either in their early careers or who were studying music at higher education level. We decided to focus on the theme of women in opera, and from here we quickly noticed how many of the female characters in opera were created by men and were often highly stereotyped, limited in scope and not representational of the actual female experience. We researched the work of poets and writers such as Audre Lorde and Maya Angelou and the writing and music of Pauline Oliveros. We became interested in how we could invite each of the women involved to share their experiences of womanhood and what it might be like to examine what our individual and collective 'voice' might be within the project.

On reflection, I see that the work we did in preparation for this project, helped to give it a strong foundation and grounding before we started the practical work in Athens. Each of us contributed to the research and thinking, drawing on our own concerns, questions and experiences as well as looking outwards for others. Although we worked together regularly within the ensemble, this research period allowed us to find our 'voice' as ensemble within this particular project – what was important to us here and how would we connect to this project individually and as an ensemble? What felt interesting and relevant to offer to the group and how should we go about making that offering? Alongside this, Evi worked incredibly hard to prepare for the project in Athens, building the partnership with Melissa, meeting the women involved and establishing and agreeing the parameters and expectations for all involved.

As someone who works regularly as a musician and facilitator, I see now how unusual it is to work in this way with a partner organisation, in this case the Greek National Opera. As an ensemble, we were in the conversations with Evi (who was also the project manager) from the very inception of the project. We decided almost everything about the project together, in partnership, and Evi always included us in any developments or changes. Much of this is down to Evi and how she works, and for me it really impacted the project and my connection to it, which felt deeply shared, in terms of knowledge, responsibility, and ownership. One small practical example of this, is in deciding the timings of sessions, Evi took the care to plan these around the programme of activity at Melissa and around the schedules of all the participants involved. But she also asked me about my daughter Wren's schedule and how the sessions might fit into and impact this. Being such good friends and knowing that Wren was just 10 months old and that I was not long out of maternity leave, maybe makes this all very understandable. But for me, it was so refreshing and felt so supportive that questions around when and how I could feed Wren were being taken into account. This small example is for me, indicative of the whole project, which gave so much space for the personhood of everyone involved, and like Breakfast Club as an ensemble, I feel that by acknowledging and supporting all of this, the project was stronger and the music better because of it.

In spending just a brief amount of time at Melissa, I can say that I believe that many of the values and priorities that I've described above feel similarly shared by the centre and the people who run it. In working at Melissa throughout this project, I was taken aback and deeply inspired by the building itself, the team who run it, the women who attend sessions and use the centre and the whole community around it.

Here, in central Athens, in a country so well known for its lack of funding and perpetual financial crisis, is a vibrant, generous, thriving community hub in a beautiful building, not only well taken care of and maintained, but cared for as a home from home for the people it is used by. Every inch of the building exudes the feelings of home and family - care, love, respect, support and nurture. It's a building you want to spend time in – there is art on the walls, fresh cut flowers, a beautiful garden and balcony, a shared kitchen with fresh tea and coffee always available and the kind of freedom and ease of being that you feel in your own home. A stark contrast to the often run down and underfunded community centres I have had experience of in the UK. It is a place for learning and personal development and there is a busy daily programme of group classes and individual lessons and mentoring. And it's a place for families, with a day nursery for the younger children of the women who use the centre and a busy and bustling central living space, with a long dining table and lots of sofas, which were always full of women and children - talking, laughing, eating and relaxing together.

The atmosphere of Melissa is one of busyness, bustle, concentration, learning, discussion, laughter, conversation. It is run by Nadina Christopoulou, who is an anthropologist as well as the co-founder of Melissa. Nadina employs a team of women to run the centre, all of whom came to Greece as migrants themselves. The political and the sense of collectivity, empowerment and of female mobilisation and activism are also clearly central to Melissa. There are feminist and activist art and slogans on all the walls and alongside language classes and coding classes, there are classes on women's rights and political debates and discussions.

It is into this atmosphere – of womanhood – that is not only supported, but also celebrated, confident, embodied and active that we came to the centre every day in the morning and the evenings to run sessions. The women who joined the project came mainly from the Middle East and North Africa, including Afghanistan, Iraq and Libya. Some were older women, others teenagers and young adults. Often our sessions would start with a small group and would then expand to include anyone who walked past and heard the singing and music. Over five days we created a programme of music that included song and poetry in Arabic, Persian and English alongside instrumental accompaniments and new music inspired by the poetry of Audre Lorde and Maya Angelou and by Pauline Oliveros' extraordinary work, 'Bye Bye Butterfly'. We performed all of this in the central communal space at Melissa to family, friends, staff and women from the centre. It was a wonderful, moving and joyful event and one in which, as Evi described in a recent conversation, she was able to feel present in every moment.

For me, this project has been incredibly valuable and important, not only as a musician but as a mother, a woman and as a human being. The project created the kind of space in which I felt fully present as a mother and as a musician and in terms of the work and content of the project, it allowed me to actively discuss and explore some of my social and political concerns through my artistic practice and within a context that felt genuinely experimental and exploratory. To be surrounded by women throughout the project reminded me of the particular qualities of listening, sharing, knowing and experiencing that are so important to me and in which it is rare to be so fully immersed. The energy and activity that arises from this is for me, visceral and enduring.

As a new mother, this project overwhelmed me and enabled me to see the challenges I'd been facing in managing work and parenting in another light. To be able to come to the centre with Wren and Jo (my partner), to sit in the workshops with Wren, alongside other mothers and their children, and to be able to play, to lead and to fully contribute to the work was amazing to say the least – moving, eye-opening and affirming. To enjoy leading a warm-up for example while the other women in the group held Wren, to sing songs with Wren in my arms, to know that I could 'be' these two previously seemingly opposing roles (mother and 'worker') was wonderful. And to also understand that, similar to the ethos of Breakfast Club, to hold and embody both of these roles didn't have to make you any less of a mother or less of a musician; in fact, it could actually bring more to the work in terms of connection and meaning. In this project, this feeling of embodiment was so strong and so vital – I was doing it and not just talking about it or imagining it! As Evi put it in our recent conversations, what we experienced there felt closer to our own lives and to our own selves. We were making our place and our space the way we wanted it to look, feel and sound.

TACHLES ART CENTRE FOR PALESTINIAN AND ISRAELI YOUTH IN HAIFA

As was mentioned in Chapter 4, Osnat Ritter is an activist, educator and researcher from Israel-Palestine who completed a Masters in 'Education: Culture, Language and Identity' at Goldsmiths, University of London in 2018. She has worked with children in Senegal and with marginalised groups in Israel and the UK. She founded Tachles Art Centre for Palestinian and Israeli Youth in Haifa.

———o———

Testimony by Osnat Ritter,
activist, educator and researcher

I have spent the last seven years, since the age of 16, working in grassroots educational projects, hoping to plant seeds for transformational change through critical dialogues, meaningful collaborations and cross-practice exchanges.

Growing up in the conflict-ridden reality of Israel-Palestine, politics is constantly, and sometimes too casually, intertwined in everyday life. Everything is political: from what you say to your sole existence has a political statement whether intentionally or not. I came to realise this quite early on, around the age of 16, when I started to be more vocal about my political views and my refusal to join the army (a mandatory obligation for every Israeli young person). Both my peer students and teachers have strongly rejected my views and saw me as a 'betrayer', a title I still carry with me every time I go back to Israel.

As a quite naive teenager, I believed I could make a change. 'There must be other people like me, who believe in peace and coexistence out here', I thought to myself, and figured I better find them and mobilise them to make a change. I therefore founded Tachles, a youth-led Palestinian-Israeli art centre in my hometown of Haifa. Around the same time I started volunteering in an educational NGO in Jaffa, focusing on Palestinian-Israeli education activism in after-school clubs and youth centres in the city.

My motivation at the time was to make a *real* change – to transform the grim and unjust political reality in my country. I soon came to realise that this change is very far away and not easily achievable. After two years of working in Tachles and in the NGO in Jaffa I felt like every step forward we had taken, we then went ten steps backwards. For example, I would feel that I had built great trust with the students, and then suddenly a war started and the classroom would be back again divided to Arabs versus Jews. We would mount an exciting event and then a week later a new racist law would be implemented. No matter what we did, the reality was always a few steps ahead of us: it always won.

I later realised that my approach to collaborative Palestinian-Israeli activism was extremely naive and did not acknowledge the profound inequalities that exist between the two. I then diverted the focus of my activism towards a more political approach;

supporting in solidarity with the Palestinian struggle against the Israeli apartheid. I started attending demonstrations on a regular basis and dedicated most of my life to activism.

At the age of 18, after receiving the official document that released me from serving in the army, I decided to move to London to further pursue my education. I felt limited in Israel and was eager to learn new skills in order to go back and implement them in my practice and activism. Since moving to London in 2013 I started my MA and worked with different organisations for alternative education with young migrants and unaccompanied asylum-seeking youth. In my research I look at youth voice and the importance of collaborating with youth to participate meaningfully in decision-making and in curriculum design for their education.

Today, five years after leaving Israel, I am very much convinced I will not go back to live there. I simply do not believe anymore that a change can be implemented from within and prefer to focus on international pressure on Israel from the outside and from movements like the BDS (Boycott, Divestment, Sanctions). This thought makes me sad and worried about the future, considering that my family is still in Israel and being away from them has been a huge challenge. Unfortunately, this has become a very familiar phenomenon in today's world where, due to globalisation, forced migration or other circumstances, families are being separated.

My views of the current situation in the world, in all honesty, are not very optimistic. I recently came to Israel for a couple of months to help my family take care of my grandmother who is ill with a terminal disease. This is the longest I have been in Israel since I left five years ago and I feel the situation has deteriorated drastically. The death toll in Gaza is growing every day; there is increasing violence against demonstrators all across the country, and more racist and undemocratic laws are being implemented. A sense of existential fear, on both sides, has been spread amongst the people. I noticed a strong feeling of apathy combined with cynicism amongst many people. I think cynicism serves as a defense mechanism, a painful way of dealing with the very bleak reality of the occupation. However, there is a growing youth movement that is doing amazing work but sadly facing police brutality at every demonstration they are organising. (…)

(…) While we might not be able to change the current situation, we can change who tells the story and I believe this is crucial. I perhaps cannot change the immigration system in the UK but I can help change the discourse by including first-hand stories of young people from a forced migration background. As the educator and theorist Bell Hooks suggests, education becomes a practice of freedom when it promotes the possibility for marginalised communities to re-name the world, tell their own narrative in opposition to mainstream narratives.

Art practice and an education that engages with art can be a substantial vehicle, a creative process, to promote small changes in people's lives. Firstly, since art is a form of therapy and self-expression, it can help as a coping mechanism and a way to channel feelings of frustrations and anger in a creative way. In many cases it can help express feelings that cannot necessarily be translated into words. Secondly, the process itself, of collaborative art-making, can help strengthen a sense of community and support amongst a group of people, forging new friendships. Thirdly, art tells a story. Through engaging in art young people get to tell their story in their own terms. But the question remains – who will listen to their story?

I therefore strongly believe in the power of art to make a substantial change in young people's lives, but I also think that in order for it to make a change outside the classroom one must think about where and to whom this art is being presented, exhibited or performed. As educators I think one of our main duties is to negotiate our authority and reflect on our role constantly in order to use our 'gate keeper' position and share it with young people, clear the stage for them to take over – and oh, they will have a lot to say!

155

with young people, clear the stage for them to take over – and oh, they will have a lot to say!

9

MOTIVATION AND VALUES OF SOCIALLY ENGAGED ARTISTS

It is clear from the earlier discussion of identity and the place of artistic engagement in mental health, prisons and with refugees, that the work of all these young artists is motivated by those values and beliefs embedded in our common humanity – respect, equality, freedom, integrity, openness, inclusion, diversity, cohesion, collaboration, creativity and generosity of spirit. Not surprisingly, each person's moral commitment manifests itself in different ways according to their different journeys. But in all cases their passion for the arts, together with their compassion for people forms the foundation of their driven sense of purpose. This chapter presents five contrasting perspectives to illustrate the different ways of finding what matters to each of the artists at this comparatively early stage of their lives.

For Maite van der Marel, whose ground-breaking work with Sounds of Change in Jordan was discussed in Chapter 8, her love of music found little fulfilment in her conventional music education. So much so, that whilst studying for a degree in Music

156

Education she felt challenged "to change the music education system". Like many searching musicians, Maite was keen to find a connection between her voice as a person and that as an artist. It was only when she came in touch with her own creativity through making and not just playing music that she felt more connected as a person. This became her catalyst for wanting to create similar conditions whereby other people, especially young people, could find their creative voice.

At the time of writing Dialectic Dee was a student on the Performance and Creative Enterprise (PACE) programme at the Guildhall School of Music & Drama. In her artistic statement she demonstrates her commitment to using poetry, especially spoken word, in different social contexts. Although she is only at the beginning of her career, she is already determined for her work to be rooted in real world issues.

In her testimony (discussed in Chapter 4), Kate Smith speaks compellingly about the important role of artists as "torch-bearers for the human spirit" in a fragmented world that has lost its sense of community. Kate is a versatile musician with sharp political and social antennae, who seeks to use music to deepen a sense of connection between people in many different social settings.

Niall Williams' testimony offers an alarmingly honest and perceptive insight into a teenage world of confusion, fighting (sometimes literally) to understand his identity in a world of young people grappling with an uncertain future. But his main vehicle for finding meaning in his life came through his engagement in music – specifically through Rap, Garage and House music. Having reached a point where he felt he was "existing on the periphery of identity, grounded by a superficial confidence", Niall found that "House music offered a well-needed window" to free him from the ravages of the previous two years. He began to find nourishment and satisfaction from music production, composing and song-writing. Getting in touch with his creative voice was a lifeline for him. So much so, that he began to open other doors for himself and gained a place at university to read Religion, Politics and Society. Subsequently he joined a music, art and fashion collective, Nine8 Collective, and together with his rapidly developing world view, Niall's music has become increasingly political and socially oriented. He is totally committed to encouraging young people to engage in creative exploration in a group as this can help them to share their vulnerability, along with raising their awareness of fundamental questions and reflections about their lives.

Finally, Lauren Reid, whilst working as Personal Development Coordinator at The Irene Taylor Trust, played a central role in supporting the participants involved in the many different projects initiated by the Trust. Not only was she always 'there' for them, before, during and after a project, but her presence also allowed the team of musicians to focus on drawing out the creative voice of all the participants. As can be seen from her testimony, Lauren is driven by an idealism rooted in a deeply held body of beliefs and values. Individual people and their lives really matter to her, and this was very apparent in her work with others.

Each of these five perspectives is rooted in a very different context, but they all share the values outlined by Lauren in her testimony: "honesty, kindness, authenticity, courage, reflection, development, creativity, equality, adventure, trust, belonging, community, flexibility, expression and understanding". Along with their passion for their art and their compassion for people, the values and beliefs of these artists lie at the heart of their motivation. It is hoped that their enthusiasm and commitment will be caught by the next generation of artists who might be inspired to become socially engaged activists determined to make a difference in the world.

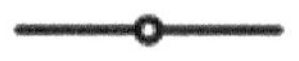

Testimony by Maite van der Marel: Sounds of Change

Reversed dreams
My musical life

If we could swim in the sky
and dive in the clouds
If we could live under water
We could turn the tide
See the moon upside down
Reverse the earth and the sun
We can change direction
Embrace the unknown

Let's immerse ourselves in dreams
Reverse what's meant to be
Let's immerse ourselves in dreams
Reverse what's meant to be

I wrote these lyrics about a year ago. Besides a reflection of my own struggles, it is an idealistic wish for the bigger world I live in. I want to challenge what we hold on to. I want us to disrupt ourselves, do things we're not used to. I wish we could truly immerse ourselves in dreams, *live* our dreams, as if it was our only reality. If we can change our perspective, we can change the world...! Did I mention I'm an idealist?

As a child I was already a dreamer. And I wanted to be different. Not in the way that I socially excluded myself: I was almost friends with everyone and I was very curious about the differences between me and my peers. But I was pretty stubborn, not afraid to stand up for my own opinion and I didn't want to follow the 'mainstream'. I had – and still have – a strong need for autonomy. I also have a problem with authority. I don't like people telling me what to do, when there is no space to be myself, when no-one cares about what I think. On the other hand, I don't like to be the centre of attention and I'd rather listen than speak. I like to step back and analyse, and I can also very easily adapt myself to others because of this.

I started with piano lessons when I was 9 years old, but as much as I loved making music, it also frustrated me for many years. Around the age of eleven I introduced myself with: "Hello, my name is Maite and I don't want to become a pianist when I'm older". Can you imagine what kind of image I must have had of being a pianist? My piano teachers put sheet music in front of me, wanted me to practice scales and didn't care much for who I was as a person. I didn't feel motivated and so tried many different teachers, thanks to my dad who took my frustrations seriously. Despite these frustrations and a strong interest in psychology and sociology, I felt there was a lot more to explore in music and so I decided to study music at the conservatory in Rotterdam, The Netherlands.

I started a bachelor in Music Education. It felt oppressive to me. I never felt I could really fit in because the system was very limited and directive. For me music was bigger than just me playing the piano. This is why I studied music education in the first place. I wanted to work with people; I wanted to put music in a bigger context, with deeper values. But the education system I faced was not at all built around that. I could feel the stubborn and idealistic tiny little Maite come to life again. I stood up for a very ambitious mission to change the music education system. I wanted to create my own path and collect more tools and techniques for a different approach and so I decided to study for a master's degree at the conservatory in Utrecht, The Netherlands.

During this master's programme I felt very insecure. Playing the piano triggered a continuous reflection on myself – and music never lies. Through very inspiring lessons from my piano teacher, who really understood me, I increasingly started to find my own voice. It was a big step for me to compose my own music and everything I played of my own felt so much more connected to me and therefore more meaningful. Nevertheless, over that period of five years I still didn't feel I fitted my image of what a musician should be like. I struggled with my musical identity. I didn't feel the need to be on stage, I felt a lot of fears and kept comparing myself to other musicians. The inner critic in me was so strong that it kept me from playing.

In this period, I also started to run projects in places where I felt creative music processes could have an impact. I truly have an indestructible belief in the power of music and endless faith in the capabilities of people. So I created a safe environment for people to explore, to go beyond the limits of what they think they are capable of. An environment free of judgments, where you don't have to conform to any image, where you can feel the synergy and invent something new together, with your own signature. I started to give people what I needed myself.

I came to realise these two worlds – work and my artistic practice – should not be approached separately. The research and learning in my work are also connected to me as a person and therefore as an artist. The urge to create became bigger and bigger. I wanted to breathe again. I needed to break through this barrier that blocked my creativity.

I started working with a Turkish singer. We both had some musical struggles and decided to compose new music together. The only goal was to make honest music – music that would come straight from the heart, transferring pure emotions to our audience. We became very close friends. We started our sessions with sometimes hour-long talks. We talked about everything, about life. Through these processes I found myself more able to open myself up in the music as well, to be more connected. My own voice and fascinations in music are now becoming more distinct. I feel more empowered through this process of connecting and creating. And even if it's not the music the whole world would want to listen to, I still feel strongly about it. It expresses my own identity. It's a reflection of my soul.

I want teenagers also to make music that really comes from within, that touches their audience, that is about real life and being put on a real stage – not played hidden in a classroom. I want people of all ages to feel the freedom to play with musical ideas, to use their imagination and to feel included in the process of creating this, to feel the power of the group. As I said before, the lack of this in my life made me want to create this for others.

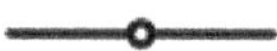

Testimony by Dialectic Dee: spoken word artist, producer, facilitator

The reason why I do my work is simple: to offer and voice my opinions on issues which matter to me and to shine a light and raise awareness on what is currently going on in the world, allowing space for my words to spark a conversation between myself and the audience, often leaving the floor open for debate and mutual exchange.

I live to create participatory, socially engaged and thought-provoking work, which has led me to discovering that my true intention and purpose as an artist is to use the arts for more than just entertainment purposes, but rather as a tool, as a vessel to positively impact others and bring about change. I feel that poetry and live music events have the power to do this. To enrich, transform and change lives.

Poetry is embedded within our everyday and even though we may not realise it at times, rarely are we wordless. We use language so frequently; everyone has their own train of thought and therefore has something to say. It's just about whether or not we find the courage to own it and to embody it, which is exactly why I write. I write poetry and hope that through running workshops and teaching poetry to others, it will encourage them to unlock, utilise and acknowledge the full potential and power of their inner voice which is so frequently overlooked. When I perform my work I never know who's going to be in the audience, who could be listening or whether or not they may be going through something similar to what I am currently experiencing. So if someone can relate or connect with my work, it inspires me and reminds me of the importance to keep on going.

As much as I write for myself, I write for my words to be spoken, to be heard, to have life breathed into them. My biggest fear is for my words to fall on deaf ears, especially if it's because people feel that poetry is not for them, or feel as if it is a foreign inaccessible language. Ironically this is how I felt after my first encounter of anthologies and page poetry, hence the reason why I chose to become a spoken word artist rather than a page poet. I don't hate page poetry, I just hate poetry that exists lifeless upon a page, poetry that only resonates and speaks to a certain type of audience.

I have a huge vision for my poetry career and where my words may take me, but for now my goal is to make poetry that is meaningful, truthful, honest and genuine to my beliefs and views. I like to write about controversial issues, the issues that people are often afraid to talk about, the issues that people shy away from, the issues that tend to go unexpressed, unrecognised and unnoticed but deserve to be touched upon.

I hope to pursue a professional career as a touring spoken word artist, educator and events producer with the hope of one day running my own outreach company. I want to create work that is refreshing and makes people think long after they are no longer in my presence, that touches and moves people in ways they could never imagine, whether that be emotionally, physically or actively. My work has always very much been people-driven as I create work for the people and therefore feed off the energy of others.

I have come a long way. However I still have a long way to go as I believe that there is always room for development and growth. Currently I'm trying to establish discipline and find balance. I have always said that 50% of my craft is writing while the other 50% of my work is performance. Therefore for me neither can exist without the other, as they both go hand in hand. So it is vital for me to treat them equally in order to become a master of my craft My poetry is an insight into my mind and the limitless potential of my imagination.

All in all I want to make poetry that is an accurate representation of the times we are living in.

Testimony by Kate Smith: singer, music leader and entrepreneur

Becoming an artist has helped me do (my) work for myself. By doing, by practicing – I create community in my own life. By sharing my practice with others (artists and non-artists), I hope to be a channel for others to do the same. My preferred vehicle is the voice, which I use in myriad ways – as a performer, as a maker, as a leader, and as an entrepreneur – to reach out to others, to cross barriers of culture, background or experience, in order to make a human connection. In my day-to-day life (at the moment) this means that some days I get to write music with people in hospital suffering from anorexia, other days with people living with anxiety and depression. Some days I raise my voice in harmony with other professional singers, others I lead workshops exploring embodiment and ensemble. And about once a year, I manage to create a temporary family by bringing together people for intensive creative residencies under the aegis of my company, Curiosa. I resist the urge to brand myself, I am content to remain difficult to categorise, a pleasure I wish everyone to enjoy.

I believe that, as human beings, we take comfort in routines, in patterns, in the recognisable. But those spaces are not necessarily the spaces where wonder can be felt, where curiosity can be entertained, or where empathy can be cultivated. I believe we find meaning when we are tempted to cast our imagination outside of ourselves, when we seek to express the intangible, and contemplate the unfamiliar.

And it's no surprise that not only does this fill us with a sense of our own power and joy in our presence on earth, but it also brings us closer to each other. By sharing our creative capacity with one another, I believe we can find the resilience to face the unknown with a little more aplomb, to imagine an alternative future with more connections, more joy, less loneliness, and less fear.

———◇———

Testimony by Niall Williams: music, art and fashion collective, Nine8 Collective

I am a twenty-two year old musician from North London. My work comprises predominantly up-tempo dance music in the vein of Garage and House, into which I have recently incorporated Rap. While I began my journey with music playing the guitar and piano as a child, my relationship with Rap began in Year 8, when I would ghost-write gangster Rap verses for a peer in my class to ingratiate and initiate him into the local gang in Queen's Crescent, which he would pay me what was then a handsome fee. Rapping remained a social hobby for me and others in my friendship circle, and my parents gave me a microphone and some software to record songs at 14; software which I in turn used from 17 onwards to produce House music, after falling in love with the dancing, emotion and euphoria surrounding the genre.

An interest in UK hip-hop amongst myself and my contemporaries blossomed under a lifestyle we had adopted – to smoke weed, stay out late with girls and get into fights at school, then later outside on the streets. What characterised this part in my life was a state of confusion regarding identity; being from a middle-class background at a diverse school where my closest friends were working class, presented a challenge of social pressure to conform to that which surrounded me. Whilst most of my friends were on the same wavelengths and conformity was not so much needed – we were relatively okay kids with much already in common, who liked to smoke and listen to music – others had a markedly different outlook on life, characterised by desire for independence. A peer once asked me how I had money to go to the cinema or play money up and I said my mum gave me money from time to time, to which he replied he made his own money. I befriended and began working with him from the age of around 13 or 14, after going to his house and seeing a thousand pounds cash in a shoebox. The desire was not to ingratiate myself with a world I was not from nor knew anything about, it was more a deep shame that this boy is independent and can support himself, perhaps even others within his family, while I am sponging off my parents. Furthermore, there was a machismo and desire for popularity which motivated this decision; making money in relation to group dynamics at school hierarchically set someone above the rest of the boys. This was particularly because being successful in making money at that age meant having some sort of respect or fear from other boys, which prevented you from being robbed or picked on at school. This respect ripples out to your contemporaries, and suddenly friends hold you in higher regard, as do girls, and this slowly branches out to older year groups at school, then to outside of the school. Hence by the age of 16 I had been clubbing and partying with older teenagers, and in some cases adults, for a couple of years, and carried myself in a different way as a result. However, this perceived respect and kudos I had developed proved fleeting and superficial as I matured.

Of course, in retrospect this is a far too-young age to become a breadwinner and cut off financial dependence from one's parents, and the reality of my peer and I was far from that of independence, or even respect from others. In being someone who upheld an air of violence or malice, one imitated these sentiments through picking on other kids and getting into fights – I very much doubt that those who were picked on by me at school hold me in any high regard or respect today, and those I fought either won and disrespected me for my victory or lost and disdained me because of it. Moreover, the use of cannabis mars the confidence one is feeling as it is synthetic, a hit provided to you by being stoned. Similarly if I make money, or hit a boy in the face, or jump in to a fight, these are temporary bursts of dopamine rewarded by synthetic or forced affirmations of respect from others. Those that showed me respect for these actions did not truly respect me; they were either scared or entertained by these actions. Thus false respect fed into false confidence, and by removing both of these elements – the malicious or unconsidered actions and the use of cannabis – one's confidence is truly left in tatters, along with one's identity. I was existing on a periphery of identity, grounded by a superficial confidence and imperative to perpetuate smoking weed as well as violent, malicious and masculine tendencies to uphold this confidence.

Perhaps reflectively House music offered a well-needed window to emasculate myself. House entered my life at a time where machismo-driven violence in my life had peaked, being victim to a knife attack at the start of my GCSEs, then a few months later going back into hospital from being glassed in the face and neck after watching an acquaintance stabbed in the stomach in front of me moments before. House and 'cutting shapes' was cool, but it was also a way of expressing yourself in a positive way, and of course historically is a counter-culture to hip-hop, formed by working-class gay communities in North America that were not accepted by their hetero-masculine contemporaries.

The years between 16 and 20 have been a cathartic process of emasculation; my familial relationships have improved, as well as my empathy, and sympathy to the victims of blind patriarchal behaviour from men, a sentiment which has found its way into my music through arriving at the telos of this journey. Attending a Sixth Form, which produced far higher achievers than my Secondary, apart from my prior contemporaries, was the first step to ushering in a less violent future. I did not fully escape these tendencies, however, and an episode just before my eighteenth birthday – caused by bad company and excessive use of cannabis – left me temporarily diagnosed with drug-induced psychosis. This was truly a wake-up call for me regarding my relationship with cannabis, and I never smoked again. The shock to my mental state also required me to isolate myself in relative solitude, following a break-up which occurred shortly after the episode, until I was ready to re-take my Year Thirteen examinations in the summer of 2016. Whilst revising for these exams and reconfiguring my mental stability I had more free time to work on my music, and reconnected with an old friend from secondary school who acted as both mentor and good friend to me as I honed in my skills in production, composing and song-writing. I managed to attain the grades required to attend a good university, and went on to study Religion, Politics and Society. At university, critical contemplation of broader, extant issues facing me, such as social pressures, existential and theological questions contextualised my individuality as part of a wider matrix; which I believe quelled my previous compulsion and obsession with how the world perceived me, and centred my thoughts more on how I perceived the world around me. During university I also nurtured my more vulnerable traits and embraced them, for strength and stoicism was no longer a currency I or my new friends primarily utilised, and the collective I joined while studying has become the perfect home for my new outlook and views to be voiced through music.

Over the past year I have joined a music, art and fashion collective called Nine8 Collective, founded by a femme (a lesbian with traditionally feminine characteristics) woman of colour. The collective has a strong ethic of empowerment and self-love, both representing and upholding underground, under-represented culture. This has had a visible effect on my music; my first exploration into merging my work as a House music producer and rapper included the lyrics 'love and prosperity, racial equality, female empowerment that is the cure / succession of ailments are poisoning cities but we push this music to settle the score'. The ailments I speak of here range across different fields; politically, dissatisfaction with government initiatives such as austerity and neglect of areas leads to increases in violent crime and feelings of disenfranchisement, the latter reflected in many of the Brexit voters from impoverished towns and cities. The social ailments include a stratification of classes, in which subconsciously we prejudice and self-segregate because we do not feel unified nor respected. Lastly, toxic masculinity and stubbornness to accept those that live in a different paradigm to the norm are rife in cities, issues I and lots of my musical friends aim to address through our music. I am of the belief that the best remedy for these issues is through positivity, a positivity which is immediate, not a positivity borne out of hope or progressive, forward-thinking, as that is illusory.

In one of my lines, I say 'my life has never been more than a Kentish slab on the pavement floor'. This line is an exploration into de-egotising oneself within an existentialist context. Earlier in the song I remark that you may see the 'usual smile on my face because it all means nothing'. This stems from my belief that there is a profound beauty to life precisely because it is meaningless. My lack of religion leads me to be sceptical of innate goodness or badness, as well as morality, as I see no transcendental explanation for these being real, existing sentiments, rather than superficial conformities constructed by humans. My idea of happiness or a state of being most satisfied is contentment, and part of this is to be content where you are, acknowledging you are no more intrinsic or detached from your surroundings than the pavements which you have walked your entire life. Furthermore, if I can be content and happy with the fact that my endeavours, however menial or concerted they may be, are essentially meaningless, then I have no greater obstacle to face.

The reason I bring this up is that if one is of similar inclination, or perhaps a completely different inclination to me, then one of the best methods to explore this is through art. In my opinion all art is existential; it is that which we grapple with to explain our understanding of life and existence. We are trying to make others feel something, tell them something or make ourselves feel something more profoundly about why we are here or what we have experienced while being here. This is extremely beneficial for young people, as adolescence is one of the hardest stages in life to navigate oneself through. Addressing these deeper thoughts will help one to understand oneself better, which is where true confidence derives itself. To have a self-constructed sense of identity and confidence founded through self-exploration reduces the proclivity to appeasing others through peer pressure in order to cultivate confidence or sense of belonging. The disorientation teens experience is to some extent an inexorable side-effect of adolescent hormones, but it is not aided by the lack of artistic endeavours embarked upon during teen years. It is the ultimate internal conflict to turn oneself inside-out in order to articulate one's internalisation of life, and how this informs one's perception of existence, through a piece of artistic work. A human is most vulnerable when connecting with or creating a piece of art, be that music, visual art, or any other medium.

Linking back to the sentiments of empowerment I try to espouse musically, one must be open to vulnerability to accept these positive facets. If one cannot explore and exhibit their inner existential anguish, how well equipped is one to understand the anguish of others, those that are less empowered or represented? Furthermore, participating in this creative exploration as a group will heighten young people's awareness that these universal questions and reflections are experienced by all individuals. To engage in a vulnerability-inducing exercise in a group can only help to promote an openness to states of vulnerability, and in turn open relationships with others and their vulnerabilities, which is one of the strongest traits one can possess.

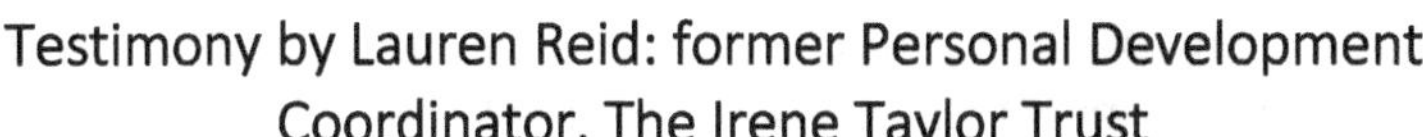

Testimony by Lauren Reid: former Personal Development Coordinator, The Irene Taylor Trust

Amongst its different activities The Irene Taylor Trust supports people to break the cycle of reoffending. Whether that is preventative or restorative, music is used as a tool to enable this. My role is to support the participants we work with during and after our music projects, by way of assisting their education, training and possible future employment. The foundations of my experience are rooted in support work and this qualifies me to go further than is sometimes required, in that if an individual is struggling with their housing, emotional health or relationships, I have the experience to know how to provide this additional support and signpost them to the right area for further support.

Whilst undergoing a BA Hons degree in Applied Theatre and Education at The Royal Central School of Speech & Drama, I began to observe and understand the complex systems and power struggles individuals navigate based on their identity or social economic status and felt stimulated to challenge social injustices. After my degree, I began working on the National Domestic Violence helpline for the charity Refuge. I then worked at the Gaia Centre as a Young Persons Community Outreach Worker for two years. This was a very formative time in my professional development as this role was new to the organisation, and a colleague and I constructed and developed the service to support young women at risk of gender-based violence. I was completely thrown in at the deep end and learnt very quickly whilst at frontline level. My cases were complex, diverse and challenging, filled with trauma and based mostly around sexual violence and children. I found out later that this was and is the main cause of vicarious trauma. I feel suffering from vicarious trauma and burn out led me to leave this role prematurely and leap into management (away from frontline work). I also had valuable skills and broad experience to put into a service being created in West London. In this service, we ran a youth centre (of sorts) with a music studio and supported NEET (Not in Employment, Education or Training) to 16-25-year-old mixed-gender participants. This is where I began to understand the complex criminal justice system and began to invite a creative element back into my work. After completing my time there, I began working as a support worker for ADVANCE Minerva alongside The National Probation Service, supporting women involved with the criminal justice system.

I grew up in London, this vibrant city full of possibilities, diversity, eclecticism, culture and above all – Art. My mother and father were punks in the 70s and from a young age I remember music surrounding our lives. The Beatles, the Stones, Neil Young, Top of the Pops; my father would play his guitar to me and write his own songs. I found music of my own via learning the piano, dancing and recording what I could from the radio. I loved collecting music and when my access to technology advanced, I realised I could download or stream anything and everything I wanted to. I'd save up my pocket money just to buy the newest CD or MP3. Music followed me through university and throughout most of my career as a sort of solace/ private place/ healer and allowed me space to breathe and think. When the role at The Irene Taylor Trust came into my life, I realised it brought together two passions of mine – people and music. This was further cemented when I realised that not unlike my own experience, music also helped others who needed guidance, aspiration, connection, space, and a sense of belonging.

On the hardest days of the work I have asked myself many times, 'is this for me'? Am I the person who should be supporting others? Have I got what it takes? In the same moment, I support someone who has walked such a difficult path in life, felt so much pain, oppression, shame, injustice, isolation, loneliness, lack of creativity, lack of self-expression, under-nourished physically, emotionally, spiritually – purely based on the circumstances they were born into. They have faced such adversity from day one, made countless mistakes but still, something, somewhere, deep within they have the courage to carry on, to survive, to ask for help, to continue. I hear it in the songs that are created and the conversations I have with them. Hope.

I value honesty, kindness, authenticity, courage, reflection, development, creativity, equality, adventure, trust, belonging, community, flexibility, expression and understanding. I have always tried to incorporate this when approaching all situations in my life, whether that is personal or professional. I try to take that forward in the work I do. To see the individual for whom they are and where they're at, and work with that – to be flexible around the fact that where they're at now might change in five minutes and to work with their beliefs rather than mine.

Sometimes someone can say something to you, or you listen and watch something but it doesn't mean anything to you at that moment. Other times the same thing happens, and you feel as though you have been hit right between the eyes. I feel like that about many people who come in and out of our lives – trajectories that collide at the right time. The same could be said for art and specifically to me, music. It has the power to heal, influence, educate and connect. I am motivated in the belief that music can be used as a vehicle to transform someone's life at the right time, when they are ready to listen. I have seen first-hand, in the work that I do how it can be the biggest protective factor against any of their vulnerabilities and tap into aspirations they never even thought they had. It can guide them along another path rather than the one they are on, better than anyone else could tell them. I am motivated by the future, a world in which I believe is attainable and how I personally can impact on it for the better through helping people find their creativity.

Through my work I have seen and listened to the hardest situations that are incomprehensible in my own life. I used to think that I needed to be stronger, that I had to shut off my emotions. For a while I was able to do that, however the violence I was hearing in my day job only manifested itself in my dreams. How do we switch off from human suffering when the whole reason you do what you do is to turn towards it and try to change it for the better?

I am at a place in my life where I am still trying to understand myself and the world. I am still struggling to find my own equilibrium. I am figuring out who I am, my limits, my boundaries and how my own inner and outer worlds co-exist.

What upsets me most is sometimes feeling as though we live in a society sick from the inside out. The pain and trauma I see in the news, on documentaries, in my professional life and the way we treat one another leaves me sometimes in great disbelief. Social media constantly bombards us with endless information which is both positive and negative. We have never been more connected and yet disconnected and are still unsure about the impact it will have on the world in years to come. We live in a world built on instant gratification with money, power and toxic masculinity driving it all. We are distracted, coerced by the things around us, e.g. sex, alcohol and social media feeding us like empty vessels, pretending or giving us a false sense of feeling fulfilled even though deep down we don't feel it. Where is this coming from? Are we so busy consuming and being consumed that we don't focus on the powers-that-be that keep us here? How are we affecting nature and our planet? What we eat, think, speak, do is affecting our development and communities whilst we are running with our eyes closed.

I recently found a Bertrand Russell quote that really spoke to me: "One of the most painful things about our time is that those who feel certainty are stupid and those with any imagination and understanding are filled with doubt and indecision." Sometimes it feels as though there are very rare avenues to turn to with these questions and I am unsure even where to start. No one wants to see the cracks in society or to hear the stories of trauma or corruption. It feels as though individuality is a little lost and if you dare to go against the grain or do something other than the 'collective' you are considered strange.

And then, in another thought, I am reminded daily of the human will to survive. I witness someone persevering against it all, I talk to someone I love, and we connect, communicate and share something. I sit in nature and marvel at a world so much bigger and greater than my own tiny little piece of it. I remember I have hope for the world. I remember things are probably better now than they ever were for some people. I believe in people. I believe in humans and their innate survival instinct, I believe in community and most of all, I believe in love.

I believe that sometimes you must take a risk in order to leap over a barrier; I believe sometimes you must knock everything down to rebuild it. I believe you must accept that sometimes you won't rebuild it and some things are greater than you and out of your control. I believe that we all fear failure, but true bravery is to acknowledge that and go forward anyway. I believe in a healthy mind, soul and body. I believe in allowing yourself the space to find out what that means to you. I believe in the small things that go unnoticed but if you stop to appreciate them, they are big. I believe the quality of the people you surround yourself with is one of the most valuable things, but also to keep connected to those individuals who may be completely different from you, but who nevertheless speak your rhythm. I believe people go through tough times and life isn't black and white, but there is a lot of messy grey and that we are all trying to figure out that part. I believe the best thing you can do for another person is to try to understand their messiness. I believe we all have a duty to ourselves to support our own mental health and by doing that we will have more to give to others. I believe in the power of community and that we are all responsible for a better world outside of ourselves. I believe in practicing what you preach. I believe in listening, advocating and supporting those who need it. I believe in supporting and empowering others to find the path for them. I believe in not judging one another or the journeys we are on. I believe what we often hate in others is what we hate in ourselves and that guilt, shame, jealousy, anger are emotions we all feel but if left undealt with, will affect us and others long term. I reference back to these fundamental core values or mottos in the work that I carry out.

10
CLARION CALL: CHALLENGE TO ARTISTS, CULTURAL AND HIGHER ARTS EDUCATION INSTITUTIONS

The main thrust underlying *Young Artists Speak Out* is that those young creatives who are socially engaged, who see themselves as activists, have something really important to say. Their voices need to be listened to and acted on by cultural leaders and the next generation of artists. **This has major implications for cultural and higher arts education institutions many of whom in the past have tended to place social engagement on the periphery of cultural practice.**

One of the fundamental challenges confronting leaders and policy makers in these institutions is how to bridge the enormous gulf between rhetoric and action, between statements of intent and practice. If socially engaged practice is seen as a vital force to be reckoned with, how do institutions intend to make this a reality where their dominant culture in the past has been resistant to change? How can they embrace change at the same time as valuing the traditions of the past?

A good starting point might be to listen and respond to the voices of the young creatives and social activists that speak so clearly and passionately about their practice in *Young Artists Speak Out*. Their testimonies, case studies, poetry and conversations provide convincing evidence of the impact they are having in their many different ways. Their energy and commitment, underpinned by their passion, compassion and sense of purpose, should provide the inspiration and example to activate other young artists.

Institutions like conservatoires *have to* become more open and receptive to the new possibilities arising from a rapidly changing social and cultural world. They *have to be* courageous enough to embrace radical change. They need to harness the dynamism and pragmatic idealism of the young activists as they articulate a vision for the future of their institutions, recognising the urgency for a change in direction and a realignment of priorities. Curricular programmes need to be reappraised, along with the mindset of those staff and students locked in a world that fails to engage with the present. This is nothing less than a major challenge to leadership and to the culture of institutions.

Of course, it is clear that 'youth voice' won't be heard, valued and legitimated by those intransigent cultural institutions who remain trapped in the norms of the past, seemingly oblivious to the new possibilities being opened up by those young people responding to the changing political, social and cultural landscape. As intimated in the Manifesto at the beginning of *Young Artists Speak Out*, the whole arts community should be engaging in an inter-generational conversation, rooted in a collaborative culture serving as a catalyst for change and action.

Such a culture would encourage the process of making connections in which the cross-fertilisation of ideas and practices and collaborative ways of learning would promote creativity and innovation. This cannot be achieved in isolation, in a silo of convention and predictability. People have to choose to work together, celebrating how their different talents, perspectives and insights can create something that transforms their practice and ways of seeing the world. It is through interaction, with its unique chemistry, that creative ideas and leaps of imagination begin to fly. Creative challenges emerge from the group responding to the unexpected. New knowledge is 'co-constructed' through dialogue, risk-taking and the shared exploration of ideas and meaning within the group. This lies at the centre of collaborative learning with 'conversation' being the engine driving the creative process. Different forms of social engagement would be integral to this culture of creative collaborative practice – one that is responsive to the challenges of the time.

Whether or not cultural organisations, especially higher arts education institutions, are ready to engage in such potentially life-changing conversations remains to be seen. But it is almost impossible for them to ignore the injustices, the social issues, the sense of dislocation and isolation arising from a political world that seems to have lost its moral compass. The arts by themselves cannot resolve these issues but they can play a significant part in enhancing people's lives and helping them to become more connected to themselves and to others. It is hoped that the evidence provided by the young creatives in *Young Artists Speak Out* demonstrates the power and scope of socially engaged and creative collaborative practice.

CALL TO ACTION

In conclusion, I will return to the fundamental questions raised in the Provocation (Chapter 2). They constitute a clarion call for artists and cultural and higher arts education institutions. Positive action will transform the culture and landscape of these institutions as well as making a significant difference to people's lives.

Let these questions be at the heart of inclusive national and international dialogues between students, emerging artists, teachers and leaders of higher arts education institutions, arts councils, major arts funding bodies, the research community and strategic organisations like the Association of European Conservatoires (AEC), European League of Institutes of the Arts (ELIA), International Society for Music Education (ISME), International Music Council (IMC), European Music Council (EMC), Youth Music and Sound Sense, the UK professional association for community musicians.

- In what ways might young activists and higher arts education institutions establish a dynamic dialogue to ensure that social engagement becomes a priority in the preparation and continuing development of artists?

- What structures and resources outside current institutions are necessary to facilitate and strengthen the social impact of young engaged activists and nurture them as potential social leaders?

- In what ways might cultural and political leaders accept greater responsibility for recognising and nurturing socially engaged artists for their commitment to shaping a more inclusive, compassionate society?

- What action needs to be taken to bring socially engaged artists in from the margins to a more central strategic position in the cultural field?

- In what ways can more young artists be galvanised to find the passion, compassion and sense of purpose to make a difference in the world?

- What action can be taken to ensure that the next generation of artists has the artistic strength, vision and motivation to create a world in which engaging in the arts enhances the quality of people's lives?

- In what ways can cultural institutions be activated to produce a socially engaged workforce that responds creatively and responsibly to the diverse challenges of a world in constant flux?

BIBLIOGRAPHY

Alston, P. (2018). *Statement by the Special Rapporteur on extreme poverty and human rights on his visit to the United Kingdom of Great Britain and Northern Ireland.* New York: UN Human Rights, Office of the High Commissioner.

Arts Council England. (1997). *Leading through Learning: The English Arts Funding System's Policy for Education and Training.* London: Arts Council England. www.artscouncil.org.uk

Arts Council England & Durham University. (2019). *Durham Commission on Creativity and Education.* www.artscouncil.org.uk/publication/durham-commission-creativity-education

Ascenco, S. (2017). *The Lullaby Project: Areas of Change and Mechanisms of Impact.* London: The Irene Taylor Trust. www.irenetaylortrust.com

Atwood, M. (2018). *Freedom.* London: Vintage Editions, Penguin Random House UK.

Calouste Gulbenkian Foundation. (1982).*The Arts in Schools: Principles, practice and provision.* A Report to the Calouste Gulbenkian Foundation on the place of the arts as part of the school curriculum in the maintained sector of education. www.gulbenkian.org.uk/publications

Cultural Learning Alliance. (2017). Briefing Paper No.1. *STEAM: Why STEM can only take us so far.* www.culturallearningalliance.org.uk

Department of Education and Science. (1972). *Teacher Education and Training.* London: Her Majesty's Stationary Office.

Dodsworth, G. (2018). Georgia's Story. In *Happiful,* April 2018, pp.38-39.

Drum Works. www.drumworks.co.uk/who-we-are/

Eddo-Lodge, R. (2017). *Why I'm No Longer Talking to White People about Race.* London: Bloomsbury Publishing.

The Irene Taylor Trust. (2017). *Annual Report, 2016-17.* www.irenetaylortrust.com

Lourde, A. (2017). *Your Silence Will Not Protect You.* London: Silver Press.

National Advisory Committee on Creative and Cultural Education. (1999). *All Our Futures: Creativity, Culture and Education.* www.culture.gov.uk/pdf/naccce.pdf

Osnat Ritter. www.springboardyouth.com

Praxis Community Projects. (2017). *Impact Report 2017.* London: Praxis Community Projects. www.praxis.org.uk

Rae, I. (2015). *The Misadventures of an Awkward Black Girl.* London: Simon & Schuster.

Renshaw, P. (1971). A curriculum for teacher education. In T. Burgess (Ed.), *Dear Lord James: A critique of teacher education.* Harmondsworth: Penguin Books.

Renshaw, P. (2005). *Simply Connect: 'Next practice' in group music-making and musical leadership.* London: The Paul Hamlyn Foundation. www.musicalfutures.org.uk

Renshaw, P. (2010). *Engaged Passions: Searches for quality in community contexts.* Delft: Eburon Academic Publishers.

Renshaw, P. (2011). *Working Together: An enquiry into creative collaborative learning across the Barbican-Guildhall campus.* London: Barbican and Guildhall School of Music & Drama.

Renshaw, P. (2013a). *Being – In Tune: Seeking ways of addressing isolation and dislocation through engaging in the arts.* London: Barbican and Guildhall School of Music & Drama.

Renshaw, P. (2013b). Collaborative learning: A catalyst for organisational development in higher music education. In H. Gaunt & H. Westerlund (Eds.), *Collaborative Learning in Higher Music Education.* Farnham: Ashgate Publishing Ltd.

Renshaw, P. (2017). *Collaboration: Myth or Reality? Through the eyes of the Barbican and Guildhall School.* London: Barbican and Guildhall School of Music & Drama.

Rosales, H. (2017). www.harmoniarosales.com

Saunders, L. & Howitt, J. (2019). *The Critical Fish.* Hull: Issue 1, May 2019. www.thecriticalfish.co.uk

Tachles Art Centre, Haifa, Israel. www.ocritter.wordpress.com/tachles-art-centre-haifa

Tambling, P. (2019). Reflections on 20 years of cultural learning in England. In Cultural Learning Alliance, *Newsletter*, 30 September, 2019. www.culturallearningalliance.org.uk

Waithe, L. https://abcnews.go.com/theview/video/lena-waithe-talks-lgbt-representation-hollywood-ready-player-537458295https://

Wigmore Hall Learning. www.wigmore-hall-org.uk/learning

Youth Music. www.youthmusic.org.uk

Youth Music and Ipsos MORI. (2019). *The Sound of the Next Generation: A comprehensive review of children and young people's relationship with music.* London: Youth Music. www.youthmusic.org.uk

ACKNOWLEDGMENTS

This book provides a platform for young artists, young creatives, to be heard. Their testimonies, their willingness to speak out and share their commitment and creative energy, has been a source of inspiration and it is hoped that this will be caught by other young artists considering to work in the area of social engagement. Role models matter, and there is no doubt that each person contributing to this project can be seen as a pragmatic idealist, whose work is underpinned by a passion and compassion that help to shape their sense of purpose and drive them forwards.

I am deeply indebted to all the artists and contributors for giving up so much of their valuable time to share their stories and experience in often very challenging circumstances. Without their compelling voices there would be no book and it is hoped that their collective message will impact on the practice of cultural and higher arts education institutions.

But for such a multi-faceted venture to get off the ground I've been dependent on the support and insight of a number of very experienced critical friends. Their knowledge and understanding has helped to verify the importance of the major issues, whilst their comments have given greater clarity and coherence to the project. My deepest gratitude goes to the following people, many of whom have supported me over many years: Helena Gaunt, Principal, Royal Welsh College of Music & Drama; Jackie Goodman, former Manager, Hull School of Art & Design; Sean

Gregory, Director, Innovation & Engagement, Barbican and Guildhall School; Matt Griffiths, CEO, Youth Music; Rick Holland, Writer and tutor, Guildhall School of Music & Drama; Louise Jeffreys, Artistic Director, Barbican; Renee Jonker, Director, société Gavgniès, and Director, New Audiences & Innovative Practice Master's programme at The Royal Conservatoire, The Hague; Sara Lee, Artistic Director, The Irene Taylor Trust; Steve Moffitt, Chief Executive, A New Direction; Jacob Sam-La Rose, Artistic Director, Barbican Young Poets; Linda Rose, Founder & Project Consultant, Music for Life at Wigmore Hall; Rineke Smilde, Professor of Lifelong Learning in Music, Prince Claus Conservatoire, Groningen, and Professor of Music Pedagogy at University of Music & Performing Arts, Vienna; John Stephens, Music Education Consultant; Pauline Tambling, former Joint-CEO, Creative & Cultural Skills; Laura Whitticase, Senior Manager, Organisational Development & Policy, Barbican; Jo Wills, Artistic Director, Drum Works.

Transforming a project into a comprehensible book requires the skill and critical eye of an editor, and I've been most fortunate to be able to rely on Ninja Kors, who has really helped to give shape to the text. I have worked with Ninja at different times over the last 20 years, both in her home country, The Netherlands, and in other European countries, and have always been impressed by the rigour and clarity she brings to any project. A very big thank-you to her.

As on many other occasions, Milena has continued to stand by my side as the project has unfolded – always patient, understanding and welcoming to critical friends and participants. Her selfless presence is a gift that I'll always cherish – thank you Milena.

ABOUT THE AUTHOR

Peter Renshaw is a writer and researcher for the Barbican and Guildhall School of Music & Drama. In 2001 he retired from the Guildhall School as Head of Research and Development, where he pioneered the innovative programme in performance and communication skills (1984-2001) and was Gresham Professor of Music (1986-93). Formerly he was Lecturer in Philosophy of Education at the University of Leeds Institute of Education (1970-75) and Principal of the Yehudi Menuhin School (1975-84).

He has always had a special interest in organisational change and in the learning and development of professional artists. In the 1980s and '90s he was adviser to a number of orchestras aiming to extend their role: for example, the London Philharmonic; City of London Sinfonia; London Symphony Orchestra; Royal Liverpool Philharmonic Orchestra; City of Birmingham Symphony Orchestra; Royal Philharmonic Orchestra; BBC Philharmonic; Royal Scottish National Orchestra, London Mozart Players; Royal Opera House and English National Opera.

Consultancies have included Banff Centre for the Arts, Canada; Sydney Conservatorium and Queensland Conservatorium, Australia; Sibelius Academy, Finland; Royal Scottish Academy of Music & Drama; the Irish Government (developing an Irish Academy for the Performing Arts); the British Council in Tanzania and the International Yehudi Menuhin Foundation, Brussels.

In addition he devised and led mentoring development programmes at the Guildhall School; Prince Claus Conservatoire Groningen; the Royal Conservatoire The Hague; the National Institute of Creative Arts & Industries, University of Auckland; the University of the Arts, London; The Sage Gateshead and Youth Music.

From 2001-02 he was Chair of the Steering Group for Youth Music's *Creating a Land of Music* and from 2001-03 he was

Moderator of the EU Socrates project, *Sound Links*, on cultural diversity in music education. In 2005, as part of *Musical Futures*, The Paul Hamlyn Foundation published his research report on Guildhall Connect, titled *Simply Connect: 'Next Practice' in Group Music Making and Musical Leadership.* His report *Lifelong Learning for Musicians: the Place of Mentoring* was published in 2006 by the Lectorate Lifelong Learning in Music at Prince Claus Conservatoire Groningen and the Royal Conservatoire The Hague. In 2008 The Sage Gateshead published his Evaluation Report on REFLECT, the Creative Partnerships National Co-mentoring Programme. His book, *Engaged Passions: Searches for Quality in Community Contexts* was published in 2010 under the auspices of the Research Group in Lifelong Learning in Music & the Arts at Hanze University of Applied Sciences, Groningen and the Royal Academy of Fine Arts, Design, Music & Dance, The Hague.

Most recently he was commissioned by the Barbican and Guildhall School to produce three research reports: *Working Together: An enquiry into creative collaborative learning across the Barbican-Guildhall Campus* (2011); *Being – In Tune: Seeking ways of addressing isolation and dislocation through engaging in the arts* (2013); and *Collaboration: Myth or Reality? Through the eyes of the Barbican and Guildhall School* (2017).

Formerly he was a trustee of the London International Festival of Theatre (LIFT), the Centre for Creative Communities, Accord International, Share Music (Chair) and Nuance Music Limited (Chair). Currently he is Chair of Drum Works and a trustee of The Irene Taylor Trust.

See
www.youngartistsspeakout.uk
for further resources.